ID084629I

Appropriately Subversive

Appropriately Subversive

Modern Mothers in Traditional Religions

TOVA HARTMAN HALBERTAL

Harvard University Press

Cambridge, Massachussetts, and London, England   2002

Copyright © 2002 by the President and Fellows of Harvard College
All rights reserved
Printed in the United States of America

Library of Congress Cataloging-in-Publication Data

Hartman Halbertal, Tova.
Appropriately subversive : modern mothers in traditional religions /
Tova Hartman Halbertal.
    p. cm.
Includes bibliographical references and index.
ISBN 0-674-00886-3
1. Feminism—Religious aspects.   2. Mothers and daughters—Religious aspects.
3. Jewish women—Religious life—Israel.   4. Catholic women—Religious life—
United States.   I. Title

BL458.H37 2002
200'.85'2—dc21   2002068811

Designed by Gwen Nefsky Frankfeldt

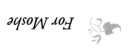

For Moshe

Contents

Acknowledgments

*In many ways, this book has been inspired by my daugh-*ters, Nomi, Racheli, and Shira. I am most grateful for their sweet love and patience when "mommy is on the computer." I hope that I have the wisdom to pass on to them the love I have for religious practice in concert with my deep respect and admiration for the fullness of their humanity.

I grew up in a home where I learned the meaning of the complexity of continuity within culture. It was a home where criticism and commitment where not considered adversaries, but rather paths to growth. Thank you to my loving parents, David and Bobby Hartman, and to my devoted siblings, Dvorah, Donniel, Adina, and Ranan, who all continue to create an embracing family for me.

I am profoundly grateful to Carol Gilligan, my teacher, mentor, and friend. After completing my doctorate with Carol, I have continued to learn from her. As we walked the streets of Jerusalem and New York, she offered her help, advice, and invaluable insights. Her theory and methodology have been the basis of much of what I have done.

My teachers at Harvard University—Kurt Fischer, Robert LeVine, and Gil Noam—were wonderful resources for me. Many of the ideas in this book began during the rich discussions we had.

I greatly benefited from my exchanges with Amia Leiblich from the Hebrew University.

I want to thank Elizabeth Knoll, the social science editor at Harvard University Press, for her confidence in this field of inquiry and for her belief that I could carry it further. I have benefited greatly from her support and good counsel.

I thank Hilary Selby Polk for editing the manuscript at Harvard University Press and for Dorothy Harman for her kind encouragement. The editing of Elliot Yagod and Elsheva Urbis of the first versions of this work was crucial and immensely helpful.

Kathryn Geismar's supportive friendship and intellectual sensibilities were seminal in developing this work. I am grateful to Nancy Richler, my close friend since childhood, for her astute comments and much needed advice.

I am deeply indebted to Jeffrey Perl for editing the manuscript and creatively expanding the research methodology. Jeffrey's uncompromising attention to detail, his editorial skills, and sound advice brought this work from a manuscript to a book.

Special thanks to Shira Wolosky who kindly gave of her time, for her warm support and encouragement. Her keen eyes and analytic skills proved invaluable at crucial junctures.

Thanks to my colleagues at the Hebrew University—Tzvi Beckerman, Steve Cohen, Menachem Hirshman, and Mark Silverman—and to other special friends—Ester Altmann, Vivienne Burstein, Chris Gilligan, Caroline Lorberbaum, Yehudah Mirsky, and Anna Nizza—who read parts of the manuscript and offered helpful suggestions.

Thanks to Hinda Hoffman, academic administrator at the Melton Center of the Hebrew University for her generosity with her time and helpful editorial comments. A hearty thanks to Valeria Seigelshifer, my assistant, for her good spirit, attention to administrative detail, and incisive substantive comments.

I am grateful to my dear friend Tamar Miller for her loving patience in reading and rereading the book. Without her friendship, tireless generosity, humor, and wisdom completing the book would not have been possible.

I thank the women whose voices fill the pages of this book, who shared their lives and struggles with me and taught me so much. The seriousness and dignity of their lives continue to be a profound inspiration to my academic pursuits and my own mothering.

This book is dedicated to my husband, Moshe, my life partner. He has continually read and critiqued the book in all of its stages with devotion. His encouragement and love have been the "manna" from which I was nourished while writing. Thank you for all that I cannot thank you for in print.

Appropriately Subversive

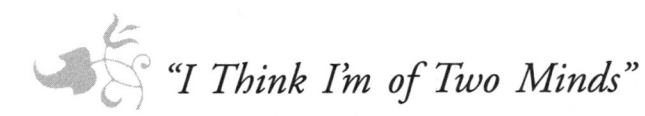 *"I Think I'm of Two Minds"*

One Friday night some years ago, I attended Sabbath services as usual at an Orthodox synagogue in Jerusalem. I felt happy and grateful to be standing next to my mother and my three daughters. Suddenly, in the midst of a prayer, my eldest daughter interrupted me to ask: "Mommy, how can you stand behind this *mechitza* and teach feminism?"[1]

Indeed, how could I agree to stand behind the curtain that separates men from women in traditional synagogues when so much of my life is dedicated to the evaluation and eradication of gender barriers? Furthermore, how can I pass on to my daughters my love of Jewish tradition without having to make sure my daughters wear a veil of self-ignorance?

The simplest solution to this particular problem would have been to leave that synagogue for one more egalitarian. In fact, this incident pushed me to establish a more egalitarian Orthodox synagogue in Jerusalem. Yet wherever we would have gone or whatever synagogue I would have established, we would have been confronted with one kind of curtain or another. I asked myself whether I needed to leave my commitment to Orthodoxy and my community in order to be consistent with what I teach and believe as a feminist. Freedom from religion, however, is not the simple option it may seem. As Luce Irigaray has noted:

> Many of us are under the impression that all we have to do is not enter a church, refuse to practice the sacraments, and never read the sacred texts in order to be free from the influence of religion in our lives . . . This does not solve the problem of how significant is the influence of religion upon culture. Thus we are all imbued with the many Greek, Latin, Oriental, Jewish and Christian traditions, at least, particularly through the art, philosophy, and myths we live by, exchange, and perpetuate, often without our realizing. Simply negating what already exists cannot make the passage from one era to the next. (1993, p. 23)

As a member of some standing in the synagogue, and prompted by my daughter's question, I asked the rabbi to reconfigure seating in the sanctuary so that the women's section would be alongside the men's section rather than behind it. Even though this change is completely acceptable in Jewish religious law, he would not even consider this alternative. "I fear," he said, "that men wouldn't be able to concentrate on their prayers and the feeling of sanctity would be lost. Besides," he continued, "Aren't women treated with respect in other aspects of synagogue life?" "How," I asked him, "could sanctity, of all things, depend on my humiliation?" What is sanctity when a mother cannot validate to herself and to her daughters the conditions of public prayer? The conversation was over.

How was I to bring up my daughters to respect and be part of a tradition that I care so deeply about when I know it requires them to pretend that such exclusions, separations—such attempts to make women disappear—have no relevance to their lives? How could I acknowledge to my daughters that they were literally kept behind a curtain for reasons that are truly not acceptable to me, yet continue to pass on my faith and tradition? This was my dilemma.

The curtain, that seemingly small barrier, symbolizes so much. It is a wall, whether in lace, in cotton, or in brick. It can be thin at times, thicker at others, but it is a constant reminder that I am educating my daughters in a system where separation and exclusion are always present. No matter what progress has taken place, this *mechitza,* or another, invisible one, is always there.

Over the years, when I have told this and similar stories to Christian friends, I have heard tales in return from what are seemingly divergent religious contexts. "With all the progress there is, women still cannot be priests," say my Roman Catholic friends with pain. They can recite the explanation that Jesus Christ was male, but this reasoning never quite resonates with them, as they pass on their traditions to daughters who can tell that their mothers remain unconvinced.

Given the inevitable overlap of cultures, today and to some extent always, mothering in culture is a matter of negotiating between truths, between loyalties and contexts, that are opposed and equally compelling. What does it take to be a "good enough mother" (see Winnicott 1986), when mothering requires knowing what benefits and disillusionments lurk beyond every conventional borderline and behind every inexplicable veil? Is there any place that mothering is not about how to manage the different curtains?

The Roman Catholic and Jewish women I interviewed for this book live on the borders and in crosscurrents of values, traditions, loyalties, pressures, and conventions. They have difficult choices to make. They do not see themselves as parenting outside of their particular cultures (if this is indeed even imaginable). Rather, they see and experience mothering as inseparable from the transmission of culture. Every mother is concerned with what traditions to pass on to her daughters and how best to transmit those traditions. Each is concerned with the ambiguity of continuity: the desire to continue, as opposed to the fear of betrayal of themselves, of their cultures, and of their daughters. As individuals, and as agents of socialization responsible for passing on cultural traditions to the next generation of women, mothers are the keepers and reproducers of culture.[2] Mothers find themselves negotiating with the "oughts" of mothering, the regulations, conventions, and orthodoxies of the traditions in which they live. As Ruthellen Josselson noted, "Throughout history, a woman's place has been defined by her society. Even when these definitions are more implicit than explicit, women are susceptible to cultural definitions of what they ought to be and sensitive to social guidelines that tell them whether they are doing a good job of being women" (1987, p. 2).

On the most superficial (which is not to say trivial) level, girls have been dressed by everyone from the editors of *Vogue* to the Sisters of the Sacred Heart, whether in uniforms, head coverings, loose jeans, tight jeans, plaid skirts, long or short skirts, high heels, or sensible shoes. These straitjackets of convention demand that mothers be concerned with whether their daughters become "good girls" through appropriate socialization. These are imperatives on mothers no less than on daughters.

Whether it is from the perspectives of modern psychologies, the landscape of liberal America, or the worldviews of traditional religious cultures, traditions try to mold and produce ideal types. Beyond appearance, what mothers are really navigating, amid the "tyranny of the shoulds," is a complex passage through or around cultural conventions. Their role is to provide daughters with the requisite tools to function, gain acceptance, and succeed within their cultural contexts. On the one hand, they must encourage the individual growth and development of their daughters' identities in their own right, as distinct from the expectations of convention. On the other hand, mothers may even be thought of as endangering their children if they do not inculcate in them the rules of social convention.

At the Crossroads of Cultures

Despite the obvious fact that all mothering (indeed all human life) takes place only within cultures, the classical psychological literature generally speaks only from the child's perspective (the daughter's experience) and ignores the mother's cultural context and central role as socializer in this context. Even where the frame of reference is that of adults, the organizing principle is the child as the receiver of care, love, neglect, or abuse. When the mother is brought into the psychological discussion, too often "she remains an object, always distanced, always idealized or denigrated, always mystified, always represented through the small child's point of view" (Hirsch 1989). "The mother" is powerfully good, bad, or silent. In each case, she is no more than a mirror in which children look to confirm their identities without interference. A mother reading these theories may find her experience entirely lost in the child's perception and the analyst's naming (Ruddick 1989, p. 38).

Against these particularities, my book focuses on mothers' subjective experiences as socializers. As is the case in other recent efforts to shift attention to the mother's self-perception, I unravel the complex choices and strategies mothers employ in coming to terms with socializing girls into their respective cultures.[3]

This book looks at mothers and mothering within tenaciously specific cultural contexts. I should state openly that I have become convinced that all cultural contexts are tenaciously specific (American liberalism, Israeli secularism, and both liberal and radical feminism not excluded). The women I interviewed for this study belong to traditional religious communities, Jewish and Roman Catholic. All are mothers of adolescent girls and are teachers in their communities.[4] The first group of women identify themselves more precisely as Ashkenazi (Jews of central or eastern European decent) Israeli modern Orthodox Jewish women, a group of which I am a member in relatively good standing. The second group I interviewed identify themselves as religious American Roman Catholic women, who likewise think of themselves as "modern." Although, I am clearly not a member of this second group, I have had deep collegial relationships and friendships with American Catholic women since the days when I was working for a degree in counseling psychology at Boston College, a Catholic institution. Many of us were mothers returning to school for an additional degree. We told our stories and talked about our struggles with tradition as women and mothers. Despite radical differences in cultural context, I was taken by surprise by the profundity of our empathy and mutual identification. I finished my doctoral program at Harvard and returned to Jerusalem to pursue my research. After concluding the interviews with Israeli mothers, I decided to return to the United States, specifically to Chicago. There I interviewed a group of modern Roman Catholic teachers with adolescent daughters of their own, in order to explore whether the experiences of the Israeli Jewish women had resonance with American Catholic women.

I am often asked why I have chosen to write about mothers and daughters, and not about mothers and sons, or fathers and daughters, or mothers and daughters and sons, and so forth. Of course all these different pairs and triangles are involved in socializing, and there are some issues that are similar. However, I was interested in the particular relationship of mothers and daughters because of the specific predicament in which women find themselves, both in their patriarchal religious traditions and in the secular psychological traditions, which portray mother-daughter relationships in a particular light.

I interviewed women who belong to religious traditions that are inherently patriarchal, even as aspects of them are changing, and that continue primarily to offer stratified roles for women and men. The women in this book are faced with mothering their daughters in cultures that to various degrees marginalize women. How do mothers resist and yet reproduce the cultural proscriptions placed on women in general and their daughters in particular? How do mothers face such a dilemma, knowing well the price to be paid by opting out of socializing their daughters, as well as the cost of passing on the culture without reflection? This is inherently a mother daughter story.

This book examines the process by which religious culture is transmitted, cultural continuity and change, and the interplay that arises between daughters and mothers. Carol Gilligan (1990a) formulates this dilemma in questions that mothers and teachers implicitly ask: "Where am I in relation to the traditions which I am practicing and teaching? and Where am I in relation to girls, the next generation of women? Are women vessels through which the culture passes?" (p. 38). These questions are critical for understanding a woman's own experience of her traditions and her role in transmitting them. How does that experience inform the mother-daughter relationship? I shall explicate in detail the central role mothers play in reproducing and transmitting cultural traditions they endorse, while simultaneously realizing the pitfalls and dangers to themselves as women and to the next generation of daughters.

All the "modern Orthodox" Ashkenazi Jewish women interviewed have a daughter over the age of twelve. For them, this string of adjectives describes their lives and multiple affiliations. The women define themselves as Orthodox in their religious practice. They accept the hegemony of the rabbinical authorities in the interpretation of the Jewish canonical texts and laws, and if they have questions regarding a certain practice, they will turn to the Orthodox religious rabbinate for resolution.

Yet they also define themselves as modern, that is, as distinct from the ultra-Orthodox women who do not have secular educations and who do not engage in almost any way with the secular world (with the exception of their use of technology). These women feel the claim of many of the values of the secular modern world and often live in tension as they attempt to find a balance between their different allegiances. They have all attended universities, meaning they have received an extensive secular education that included at least some introduction to psychology, teaching methods, curriculum design, and adolescent developmental issues, even if they specifically teach religious subjects in schools.

Moreover, unlike their own mothers, these Jewish women feel committed to tenets of feminism in one way or another. Many of them have been exposed to women's studies or have simply connected, by virtue of affiliation, with part of the Western ideal of women's value and rights. Along with the struggle to maintain strong religious affiliation, this group of women is particularly attached to the feminist vision of self-determination. Although they adhere to rabbinic authority in terms of what is permissible practice, they do not passively accept the rabbis' dicta, but often put enormous pressure on them for changes. An interesting dynamic is generated, as the rabbis "must" take their views into account, for these are not a fringe group. In fact, the religious communities trust their daughters' education to the women I describe. Without apology, one of the women told me of a request she had made to the rabbi of her community for women to carry the Torah during a festival: "I have six children. I have lived in this community from its onset—I have proven my loyalty. Now [the rabbi] must answer my question."

The American women I interviewed are middle-class Irish Catholic mothers of daughters over twelve. They are also college graduates and teachers in their parishes or in the Catholic school system. They too define themselves in terms of multiple identities. They attend church regularly and educate their daughters within Roman Catholicism so that they will adhere to the basic tenets of their faith and practice. Most of the women choose to send their daughters to

Catholic girls' schools, and those that do not send their daughters to Sunday schools. Yet feminism is a serious issue with which they feel they have to and want to contend.

They all pointed to the many changes in women's participation that have occurred since they were children, including the opportunity to be Eucharistic ministers. Elizabeth said:

> When I was my daughter's age, women could not be altar servers or Eucharistic ministers. We could proclaim the word of God, and I did, but in my cultural background [Italian] feeding others is an example of service. It is a way to nurture a relationship, just as Christ often ate with his friends. That was what I wanted to do. I felt as if my need to minister was cut off at a point predetermined by someone else. We still can't be priests, but we come pretty close!

They could find few words to justify the fact that ultimately women can never become priests. Some believed it was a matter of time, and that rules would have to change. Others were more skeptical. All felt, however, that the issue demanded and deserved attention. They did not accept, as their mothers had, fixed "truths" about women's roles in the church.

This particular predicament of women at the crossroads of cultures was movingly expressed by Kathleen, one of the Catholic women I interviewed:

> I have been conscious of the need for people to be seen as people all of my life, I guess, and early on I discovered that women were not really considered human. So most of my work has been in helping women—young and older—to see themselves as fully human with a life to live, as only they can live it, as they are called to live it just simply by being alive. My religious heritage is rich in the work for social justice, writings about the dignity of the human person, examples of women who have lived lives of courage and brilliance.
>
> The issue has always been how do we hold ourselves accountable to those who have led the way? How do we illuminate the wisdom of our

foremothers so that their lives can be a beacon for all of us? How do we insert ourselves as women—our voices, our experience, our stories, our very physical presence—into the forefront of church and society? So, while "feminism" has become a word that is used disparagingly in church circles, I claim it as my own and do not apologize. I work now at the center of the diocese, and I consciously ask questions from the perspective of women who do the work—ask questions about what we are teaching and how we are teaching and how does it affect girls as they grow and develop. How does our work affect women as they meet the challenges and opportunities of life? I think asking questions is my task. I believe that those who ask the questions help to frame the answers. I try to be appropriately subversive—or as Emily Dickinson said in one of her poems: "Tell all the truth, but tell it slant."

Like many others I interviewed, Kathleen sees herself both as deeply traditional and as challenging the tradition, or at least as pressing it to its limits. She does this not as an outsider, but from a position of strength within the Church, however uncomfortable.

Methodology

As mentioned earlier, the mothers of both groups I interviewed are all educators. They are keenly aware of the difficulties of balancing the different cultural components of their identities and of transmitting them to the next generation. They are also all university-educated at the graduate level. Their interaction with secular culture forms a central part of their lives. There are, therefore, many similarities between the groups; yet I am acutely aware of the particular cultural differences between them as well.

Comparative studies run the risk of making connections where there are none. I, too, have been privy to cheerful ecumenical comparisons of Judaism to Christianity ("Passover is the Jewish

Easter"). Following what David Hollinger calls "radical contextualism," comparative studies certainly raise serious questions. Radical contextualism claims that social and cultural phenomena can be understood only from within. Their particular features cannot be translated without being distorted into an abstract conceptual scheme. (There are those who would say not only distorted but even violated.) Extreme structuralists, however, assume that in order to understand a cultural phenomenon one must get at the root of the structure that underlies it, which is shown by other cultural manifestations of that same structure. Clifford Geertz, in spite of his assertion that "all knowledge is local knowledge," has, over time, qualified this assertion:

> The uses of cultural diversity, of its study, its description, its analysis and its comprehension lie less along the lines of sorting ourselves out from others and others from ourselves so as to defend group integrity and sustain group loyalty than along the lines of defining the terrain reason must cross if its modest rewards are to be reached and realized. This terrain is uneven, full of sudden faults and dangerous passages where accidents can and do happen and crossing it or trying to does little or nothing to smooth it out to a level, safe, unbroken plain, but simply makes visible its clefts and contours. (1985, p. 119)

In order to avoid the uneven terrain and dangerous passages, I have located myself on the continuum between the primacy of local knowledge and the structuralists' claims (cf. Levi-Strauss, 1972). "People are meaning-generating organisms; they construct their identities and self narratives from building blocks available in their common culture, above and beyond their individual experience" (Lieblich, Tuval-Mashiach, and Zilber, 1998, pp. 8–9). I share with ethnographers a deep sense of how culture frames human action and expression. As Meredith Gall, Walter Borg, and Joyce Gall observe:

"Ethnographers assume that what makes human beings unique as a species is the influence of culture in their lives, and that the most important difference between groups of people is their culture" (1996, p. 609). On many levels, belonging to one group ultimately makes one a stranger to others. "The stranger has contacts with others, and these contacts may be intensive and even intimate but he or she cannot penetrate the group itself or blur his or her separate position" (Lomsky-Feder 1996, p. 234).

I am skeptical, however, that such cultural differentiation eliminates any sort of communication. There is also the possibility of listening, of learning, of having empathy, and of understanding one another without pretending that one has no particular or separate identity. In fact, according to Geertz:

> To live in a collage one must in the first place render oneself capable of sorting out its elements, determining what they are . . . and how, practically, they relate to one another, without at the same time blurring one's own sense of one's own location and one's own identity within it. Less figuratively, "understanding" in the sense of comprehension, perception, and insight needs to be distinguished from "understanding" in the sense of agreement of opinion, union of sentiment, or commonality of commitment . . . We must learn to grasp what we cannot embrace.
>
> . . . Comprehending that which is, in some form, alien to us and likely to remain so, without either smoothing it over with vacant murmurs of common humanity, disarming it with to each his own indifferentism, or dismissing it as charming, lovely even, but inconsequent, is a skill we have arduously to learn, and having learnt it, always very imperfectly, to work continuously to keep alive . . . (1986, p. 274)

My challenge, therefore, was how to grasp the lives of the Catholic women whom I could not embrace. Cultures are in fact incommensurate. Yet to abandon all sense of common expression of mothers I believe would be both self-defeating and unnecessary. Theoretically, of course, I could have followed Helen Gardner (1959), who says: "Professor Trilling's suggestion that to suppose we can think like men of another time is an illusion, seems to assume that we can think like men of our own time, or indeed like anyone else" (p. 34).

This position brings healthy skepticism to a level of absurdity, making it virtually impossible to speak of anything or anyone. I acknowledge the humility needed in talking about other people. Within my own tradition, I understand the nuances, gestures, large and small claims; however, as an onlooker in the group of Catholic women, I did not want to assume expertise. There was, however, for all the cultural difference, also great cultural intersection. The murmurs of common humanity have actually gotten very loud in the world when people, like the women I interviewed, have in common similar syllabi of psychology courses, teaching degrees, familiarity with feminist theory, and membership in patriarchal religions.

There is a common situation despite the different content and manifestation. This common ground and mutual recognition became the basis of the methodology here, as I found that I could use this very recognition to generate a productive circularity (not one merely self-affirming and tautological). When, after interviewing the Jewish women, I began to interview the Catholic mothers, I never pretended to be merely a neutral observer with no identity of my own. I made clear my own cultural situation as a feminist modern Orthodox Jewish educator (cf. Fontanna and Frey, 2000).

I began the interviews of the Catholic women in America with open-ended questions identical to those I asked of the Israeli mothers, questions about them and their daughters. These questions reflected many of the similarities between the American and Israeli groups—for example: "Would you tell me about your relationship with your adolescent daughter?" "What are some of the things you speak about?" "What are some of the things you do not speak about?" "Are there things that you wished you could speak about but for some reason do not?"

Once we had established a rapport and an understanding of my project, I then asked them to contemplate some of the Israeli women's responses to specific issues that reflected their particular Jewish religious experience. I did this through "trigger questions," by which "researchers choose small written portions that may reflect views on issues close to what they want to investigate and ask the informants to react and express their own opinions" (Shkedi 2002, 11). I read, for example, passages describing how some of the women struggled with the different commitments they had as mothers to aspects of their daughters' development. I read them sections where they talked of the clash between their Jewish religious affinity and their personal knowledge of their daughters' well-being, such as in issues around sexuality, homosexuality, women's religious roles in Judaism, and their definitions of a "good Jewish girl." I read them portions in which certain mothers felt they had come to a juncture where they felt their daughters would be in danger if they behaved as their religion expected of them, but could not figure a way out. I shared with them excerpts in which the women abdicated their roles as socializers to their husbands or their educational institutions. In addition, I read parts of the narratives of a mother who felt she had to leave teaching in order to be honest with herself as a woman and a person. I asked, "Is there a part of this Jewish woman's narrative that you relate to, that resonates with you in your own life?" If there were comparisons to be made, each Catholic interviewee expressed them herself. I was wary of imposing my "dominant discourse" on them (Sciarra 1999), or of overvoicing them, not being able to hear them in their particular cultural voice. This would result in my imposing my own categories, theories, and worldview on my interviewees. I could not and did not assume that I knew their culture, their language, and their symbols in the same way I knew mine.[5]

This modest approach of questioning also offered an opportunity to expose differences.[6] My hypothesis was that there would be similarities (or else I wouldn't have chosen to interview this particular group of women), but I decided to seek resonance rather than clearcut comparison.

I found that the feelings of affinity, in spite of the differing and, in some ways, radically opposed orthodoxies, were once again very powerful. The Catholic women were often enthusiastic, at times agreeing wholeheartedly with what the Jewish women had said, but at times disagreeing, because of (as they pointed out) the width of difference in context.[7] In Hans-Georg Gadamer's terms, the women engaged in "fusing the horizons"—the interviews informed one group about the other, and I offered a context in which they could integrate each other's experience into their own field of references. I did not anticipate the extent to which the words of one group would reverberate in the hearts of the other.

The Catholic women often laughed or cried in their moments of identification. Ann's response to hearing a passage from an Israeli's interview is typical: "I'm very grateful to hear that, because again, that's why what you're doing might be very important, because you do these things in isolation and you don't know that others, of whatever faith, are coming to the same thing."

In this book, I do not usually repeat the passages from the interviews with the Jewish women that I quoted to the Catholic women. I am trusting to my readers to recall that whatever comparisons between traditions are made here were made by the interviewees themselves and, moreover, to understand that my theoretical assumptions are those of qualitative rather than statistical research. I am not presenting these women, of either religion, as representative; they are, in this study, representing themselves.

What I say about the Church and canon law is almost always as seen from the interviewees' perspectives. They opened their homes, their faith, their hearts, and their struggles to me. In this world I was a novice anthropologist. In contrast, the Jewish women generously shared with a "neighbor" aspects of their mothering and lives. In other words, I live with Miriam, and I visited with Mary.

In selecting women to interview, I looked for multifaceted individuals who define themselves in terms of the diversity and complexity of their cultural affiliations. As a mother of daughters and as a former teacher of adolescent girls in the Orthodox tradition, I was aware of the fears that the women might have in speaking about the very place where values and beliefs clash in their lives. Through analyses of the interviews, I began to uncover how mothers struggle with socially determined expectations and individually constructed meanings. Motherhood involves a complex negotiation of shoulds— expectations and desires variously experienced as internal, external, and in places in between.

Mothering and Tradition: Spheres of Conflict

In this book, I address the predicament of mothering in patriarchal religious cultures by addressing the following questions: How do women experience their tradition in light of seemingly contradictory commitments? How and where do they give expression to these thoughts and feelings? How are these tensions manifested in their roles as keepers and reproducers of their culture? In what ways do their perceptions of their roles as transmitters of a culture negate some of their deepest convictions as modern women? Do they see themselves as passive collaborators in a patriarchal system or as active agents of the transformation of tradition itself, or is this a false dichotomy? How do their complex experiences as agents of socialization affect their intergenerational relationships with daughters and students?

The discourse of mother-daughter relationships is informed by negotiation between both internal psychological and external cultural imperatives. Besides the particular religious dimension of their conflicts, the women interviewed share with other mothers the tensions raised by the "shoulds" of modern psychology. A major theme in mainstream psychology is the need to raise independent children, who, in order to gain their independence within the appropriate model for development, must eventually leave their "original love objects" for various adult significant others and different role models.[8] Despite much recent work in relational psychology, this "ought" of independence remains pervasive. In other words, for children to grow, mothers must be outgrown.[9] Mothers' task in life is achieved and the goal of their relationship with their children is realized only after the dependency relationships they form are terminated.

Nancy Chodorow (1978, 1989, 1994, 1995, 1999) dedicated much of her work to reframing the psychoanalytic story of the mother-daughter relationship. Contrary to the widespread elision of the mother, she insists that "from a feminist perspective, perceiving the particularity of the mother must involve according the mother her own selfhood" (1989, p. 104). While she accepts the basic psychoanalytic structure of theorists such as Mahler and Blos, she challenges it by transforming its implicit negative characterizations into positive ones, as she casts this relational characteristic of prolonged, preoedipal attachment of girls to their mothers in a positive light.

Janet Surrey and her colleagues at the Stone Center have also revised the description of the mother-daughter "war zone" relationship as a positive context in which both partners can grow and develop in tandem. This kind of mutual empowerment, Surrey holds, is the source of women's self-esteem.[10] However unwittingly, this approach may leave mothers asking, "What is wrong with me?" if the relationship is not felt to be mutually empowering.

Neither independence nor mutual harmony is an ordinary daily occurrence. Certainly neither is obvious nor even desirable, yet the women interviewed felt pressured and judged by the model of the "ideal mother." They were familiar with these dictates and "knew" not to be the suffocating and overwhelming "MOM." "I should be happy that she loves her teacher so much and confides in her," said Sima. Nevertheless, she admitted to experiencing difficulty with this development: "I should be happy that she is able to have relationships with other adults . . . but I feel jealous. Of course I don't say anything to her." I cannot help but ask what kind of rules Sima adheres to that cause her to experience discord between what she should feel like and what she actually feels, eliciting a response such as, "Of course I don't say anything to her."

Another dominant message mothers receive from the psychological Zeitgeist is their fateful responsibility for their children's future defects. Although many of the following statements have been somewhat modified by recent research, their overt and covert primacy remains.[11] Mothers of anorectics are "controlling, perfectionist, frustrated and nonconfrontational." "Failure to thrive" is attributed to "maternal neglect."[12] The mothers of autistic children are cold and rejecting (see McDonnell 1998). Schizophrenics have a schizophrenogenic mother. Maladjusted children lacking "proper ego strength" are creations of the "octopus mother . . . unwilling to hand her child over to other people" (see Jones 1998).

Paula Caplan makes an especially interesting point by comparing the destructive stereotypes of mothers to ethnic and racist denigration. Even a society that has rid itself of such deprecation feels entitled to cruelly mock mothers: "It remained acceptable to say venomous things about Blacks as long as they were Black mothers or about Jewish mothers, Italian mothers, Catholic mothers, funny old grannies, or mothers-in-law, . . . and it is a terrible thing to be a mother and know that you are expected to find them funny, that you are not supposed to be deeply hurt by them, that to be hurt is to be overly sensitive or ridiculous" (1998, p. 131).

Real mothers make choices for themselves and for their daughters in the context of these stereotypes: "I do not want to be one of those mothers!" Shoshi told me in an interview. Havva expressed guilt and remorse over her perceived inability to meet the demands of such a model—the selfless mother and the woman without need—and recognized this as an issue in teaching her children: "I know I shouldn't have such agendas for my children . . . I don't like that part in me." Even traditional women today, have an expectation that they can offer the same opportunities to their daughters that they do to their sons. They should desire and provide the same resources—both emotional and social—for their children, regardless of gender. Yet this hope encounters many obstacles, internal and external. Within certain contemporary communities, this demand for egalitarianism in upbringing is centered on education, where centuries of inequity and gender segregation have resulted in distinctly unbalanced curricula for boys and girls. Today this inequity receives much attention in the world of Orthodox Judaism. Until recently, women have been excluded from the traditional realm of Talmudic study, considered the pinnacle of Jewish education.[13] Only in the last two decades have women begun to gain access to this kind of learning (which even today often remains inaccessible to most). Strikingly, a new "ought" has developed. Now a modern Orthodox Jewish mother feels as though she should provide her daughters, as well as her sons, with a Talmudic education, yet also feels ambivalence about doing so. Sima expressed this dilemma quite strongly: "It is very important for me that my sons study Talmud, but I do not feel that way about my daughters. I know I shouldn't [feel that way], and it goes against what I thought I believed in, but this whole issue arouses primordial reactions that are just there." Here traditional educational values and contemporary feminist platforms collide. This mother is surprised to find conflict emerging in her expectations for her daughter's education. This discordance involves a complex interchange between at least two distinct pairs of cultures—that of feminism and a particular religion, and that of modernity and tradition.

Women find themselves subject to more than one system of "shoulds" when multiple cultural currents converge at a single point. These Jewish women are rooted and struggling within multicultural contexts, in particular the traditional framework of their culture and religion, and the modern secular ambience of Western thought and culture. This conflict takes hold in a number of areas, even though certain steps forward have been made in education.

Similarly, there have been inroads into equal access to Catholic canonical learning. In the Catholic world, women have been able for the past thirty years to receive a religious education in the seminaries (in fact, women can now be seminary teachers). However, with respect to religious authority, the learning that these women acquire does not invest them with the power to interpret authoritatively or decide cases of law. In both Catholicism and Orthodox Judaism, the clergy is all male. In addition, in the key performative aspects of ritual in both Orthodox synagogues and Roman Catholic churches, women generally are assigned spectator roles.

Sexuality is another problem area for traditional mothers to negotiate. Both religions' specific norms regarding "healthy" and "appropriate" adolescent sexuality frequently stand in stark contrast to Western sexual norms (see Fine 1992). (Western culture also has its own orthodoxies, as Susan Bordo [1993] shows when she enumerates secular culture's many impositions.) One woman I interviewed, Yehudit, expressed a relatively unenthusiastic but accepting stance on the sexual norms in her Orthodox community: "There seems to be some kind of ideal scenario . . . A good girl is really not terribly interested in the whole business until it actually happens . . . meeting boys, sexual attractions, choosing a husband. I would be happy if she were to go out more. I haven't discouraged her going out. I think it is something that needs practice. But a 'good girl' basically has her mind on other things . . . [such as] *yirat shamayim* [fear of heaven, piety], doing well in school, getting good grades, matriculating, doing good deeds."

Bruria, cognizant of differing views on sexuality and love, found herself addressing the implications both of Western society's permissiveness regarding sexual love independent of marriage and of the Halakhic (Jewish legal) norm of sex only within the framework of marriage: "We are speaking of two conflicting frameworks. The Halakhic framework looks positively on relationships between men and women, but only within the confines of marriage.[14] Sexuality is beautiful, but only within the marital framework . . . The Western point of view tells us that meaningful, loving relationships between men and women are possible outside of marriage. These are two standpoints. Each has its own logic, its own truth, . . . but one has to make a choice."

For the Catholic women interviewed, the question of birth control (see Greely 1990 and Dillon 1999), both for themselves and possibly for their daughters, was a primary focus and served as a constant source of struggle when dealing with the authority of tradition invested in the Church.[15] "Even though I am prolife," says Seana, "the preoccupation in our tradition with sexual matters is crazy." In frustration, she adds, as though addressing the clergy: "Don't talk to me about birth control. Give me a break! What do you know? You're sitting up with your little hat on . . . You don't have a clue. Every priest should be required to live one month in a family, and someone in the family has to have one of those really bad throw-up viruses."

Jacqueline, sharing the experience of isolation and guilt regarding her decision to use birth control says: "I have told one other person in my whole life that I had my tubes tied. I'm not proud of that, but

I had no choice . . . I thought I wasn't a good mother because I had all these children, and I couldn't do a good job with any of them, so I had no choice."

How women and, more specifically, how women as mothers and teachers define themselves and their relationships with respect to these Western psychological and religious conventions is my primary interest. Throughout the interviews, I heard women's expectations of themselves, their expectations of and for their daughters, and finally how their expectations for their daughters reflected back on themselves. There is very little neutral space in which mothers can meet their daughters. Nearly every experience is mitigated by culturally specific meanings, associations, and regulations, which mothers must eventually endorse, reject, resist, or rebut in the socialization of their daughters.

The Good Enough Mother and the Good Enough Daughter

Sara Ruddik (1989) describes the socialization (conformity, conceal- ment, and accommodation) of members of cultures as learning the "mother tongue." She claims that social groups require that mothers shape their children's growth in acceptable ways. "Children learn from their mother a 'mother tongue,' a sense of what can be named and what must remain secret; what is unavoidably given, and what can be changed; who is to be feared and whose authority is only a sham" (p. 35). While much recent attention has been focused on developing an adequate description for the socialization of the "good girl," less attention has been given to what this experience means for mothers. Indeed, women as mothers are subject to sets of "objective" criteria and norms similar to those of girls moving into adolescence. Carol Gilligan explores the relationship between the psychic pro- cesses of girls and women, and the world of culture and traditions.[16] She demonstrates that adolescent girls experience a "silencing" of that part of themselves that does not speak the "good girl's" language. According to this theory, adolescent girls undergo a repression of spontaneous feelings and emotions that do not coincide with an objectified ideal of girlhood. This perspective contextualizes development with respect to the generally accepted norms and beliefs of how girls should appear, what they should say and do, and what they should know, and what for them would constitute dangerous knowledge. During adolescence these normative ideals are felt as a chilly wind. Carol Gilligan uses this metaphor to describe a girl's coming of age in a patriarchy:

> The wind of tradition blowing through women is a chill wind, because it brings a message of exclusion—stay out; because it brings a message of subordination—stay under; because it brings a message of objectification—become the object of another's worship or desire, see yourself as you have been seen for centuries through a male gaze . . . [T]he message to women is: keep quiet and notice the absence of women and say nothing. (1990, p. 26)

In order to adopt the prevailing ideals of the adult world, adolescent girls become alienated from their deepest experiences and perceptions. They have to stop "knowing what they know" because their knowledge is potentially subversive to the social world they are preparing to enter. The penalty for resisting socialization at this stage is greater than during childhood, and the pain of nonconformity is more acute.[17]

What can be learned from Gilligan's understanding of adolescent girls' painful losses and their consequences? Do girls' experiences illuminate those of mothers in their own process of socialization? Must not mothers, too, cease to "know themselves," be "self silencing," and experience "loss of voice" in order to meet the pressures of socialization and of socializing their daughters? Mothering, after all, is a dynamic process, not a static state.

The interviews reveal a cyclical process of socialization that includes three major relationships: First, we find the mother *as a woman,* facing the orthodoxies of her life and experiencing the pressure to meet the normative requirements of society. We see the effects these demands place on her as an individual. Second, there is the woman *as a mother,* who asks herself what it means to be transmitting social and cultural norms to her daughter. What effect will these norms have on her daughter as an individual and as a member of the community? How much can and should she as a mother demand? When is her daughter a good enough girl? And finally, each mother finds her own *reflection in her daughter.* The success of her daughter's socialization and well-being measures her own success as a mother. If her daughter is a good girl, does that mean that she herself is a good mother? Or conversely, if her daughter is a good girl, has she failed her daughter by helping to integrate her into an orthodoxy that was not created by or for women? Or then again, if her daughter rebels against the societal norms, does this suggest that she as a mother has failed in some other way? And if so, by whose standards? Must mothers conform in order to gain the rewards of being a "good enough mother," and if so, how?

Ann comments on the situation women find themselves in when they try to answer these questions:

It's never completely comfortable. I can make choices in terms of "I want to do this or not." I can choose to separate myself from a situation [when] I feel "I don't want to deal with this or I don't want to be associated with this." But, no, I have to keep asking myself if I am abdicating, and I think that the question that all of us who are women in the Church have to ask ourselves again and again is, are we compromising? In so many ways I am powerless. My yelling and screaming is not going to change things. My quitting is not going to change anything. It's really so frustrating. I put myself through that all the time. I have a responsibility here . . . There are new challenges all the time, depending on how the power structure itself shifts, and it does. I think you have to keep asking that question.

There is a strong temptation to the either/or, as if admitting any constraints means denying power and agency altogether. But the relationship to constraints is highly nuanced and complex and cannot be reduced to one or the other unitary position. Despite feelings of powerlessness, Ann's attitude does anything but corroborate a theoretical position that strips women of agency. "I have," she asserts, "a responsibility here."

Women as mothers make uncomfortable choices regarding the socialization of their daughters and thereby consciously determine the prospects of the next generation. Women ambivalent about their identities as mothers frequently respond by perpetuating a cycle of silence. Anxious to demonstrate her proper evolution from "good girl" to "good woman" to "good enough mother," such a mother makes sure that the cracks in the system remain hidden and thereby repeats the process of silencing and the feeling of powerlessness. The ensuing mother-daughter relationship may sometimes involve two silent partners, two voiceless social abstractions: a good girl and a good enough mother—where even the good enough is never good enough.

One question that arises from this cyclical process of socialization is, how are we to understand silencing? Are mothers to be blamed for the perpetuation of social orthodoxy "oughts" they themselves rebel against and reject? Or is this, too, a problematic position, and are there other options available? Several theories respond to the question of why mothers silence both themselves and their daughters. Some argue that their daughters' budding sexuality and vibrancy are threatening to adult women, as a reminder of their declining sexuality, or that, in becoming mothers, women deny their sexuality and, therefore, expect their daughters to do the same (cf. Friday 1977).

These explanations, however, reflect a youth-centered perception of beauty and sexuality that one would hope a feminist would reject.

E. Ann Kaplan suggests that the archetypal mother in patriarchal societies attempts to satisfy her need "for power that her ideal function prohibits. She may also project onto the child her resentments, disappointments and failures for which the child is also to suffer" (1992, p. 48). In this view, mothers repress their daughters because they themselves were repressed. They transfer their subjection to their husbands to subjugation of their daughters and therefore continue the cyclical pattern of repression and silencing even after their ascent to a supposed position of power and influence. The implicit assumption has been that mothers are somehow failing daughters by opposing their daughters' potential vitality and by not revealing their honest critique of the norms of patriarchy.

These theories do not adequately recognize the possibility that mothers suppress the voices of their daughters in order to protect them from the consequences of nonconformity of which mothers are only too aware. The daughters lack the experience to know these consequences. Terri Apter (1990, p. 162) claims that "much of the mother's well-publicized intrusiveness comes from a knowledge that her daughter's sexuality opens her to a new kind of vulnerability of which the daughter herself is probably unaware."

In order to assure and protect her daughter's place in society, a mother may feel required to silence her individuality. Judith Herman has also claimed that the mother must initiate her daughter into an inferior position that is similar to the one the patriarchy grants her as a woman. "Mothers today must socialize their daughters into a female proletariat. This is an inherently conflictual task. The mother, herself dependent and inferior, has the job of preparing her daughter for a life of dependence and inferiority . . . She must teach her daughter to please men—that is, to be 'feminine' and to serve them, that is, to do housework . . . To protect their daughters mothers are often forced to be their daughters' jailers" (Herman and Lewis 1989, p. 144).

Gilligan, in addressing the issue of silencing (1990a), posed the question of whether "women have forgotten girls, having silenced the girl within themselves." She observed in her research that girls felt "favored by their teachers and were praised by their parents when they dissociated or dissembled" (Brown and Gilligan 1992, p. 218). She suggests, however, that when women truly listen to girls, they "find themselves drawn by girls' voices into remembering their own adolescence and . . . recall their own experiences of disconnection or dissociation at this time" (ibid., p. 224).

My interviews with mothers also show that women have not forgotten what it is to be a girl, but on the contrary, because they remain so cognizant of the painful memories of adolescence, they at times silence their daughters and themselves as a means of protection (see Apter 1990). The choice facing mothers is not as simple as a choice between whether to expose their daughters to the danger of dressing in immodest clothing—thereby arousing the anxiety and wrath of traditional society—or to dress them in the wardrobe prepared by and for the patriarchal system. Rather, in protecting their daughters, mothers demonstrate a conscious struggle with their relationship to tradition. This book will bear testimony to that struggle and, by resisting the dichotomy of silencing versus protecting, will illuminate how mothers in fact move along a continuum of silencing, protection, confrontation, and initiation.

I address the consciousness with which mothers negotiate their commitments. Their willingness to tolerate ambivalence and to make difficult choices among competing goods or values is not a sign of bad faith or passive collaboration with a patriarchy that continues to frame their lives. It is an expression of their awareness that mothering within culture has its inherent beauty and pleasures, as well as severe limitations, sacrifices, and pain. The cost of leaving is great, but the price of staying is so high. The dilemmas remain acute. The pain remains great. The options are excruciating and lead ultimately to barriers between mothers and daughters and between the mothers themselves, which in the women's current cultural situation are not resolvable. The voices of the women, however, are not those of indifferent, passive victims, but of active, thoughtful individuals whose lives are informed not only by drives and motives of which they are unconscious, but also by conscious choices and the awareness of what it means to gain or lose voice and to gain and lose relationships.

CHAPTER TWO

Ritual Observance and Religious Learning

"*I was told that I could say publicly whatever was* written in the book I received. I went home and opened it. Its pages were blank! *I am allowed to be silent.*" With these words Bruria, a religious feminist in Jerusalem, recalled a traumatic incident from her past that captures for her the prevailing Orthodox attitude toward women's place in public religious spaces. During a bingo game, as it happens, she had won a book that appeared to be a standard religious text, and she told those present she would accept the prize on the condition that she be allowed to talk about its contents publicly in the synagogue. To her surprise, the men (the *gabaim,* synagogue ushers) immediately agreed, but, eyeing one another, they asked her not to open the book until she got home. Only later did she discover that the text was actually a hardcover notebook filled with nothing but blank pages. She spoke of the incident with bitter sarcasm, and it was obvious that in retelling the story she could feel some of her original humiliation and rage. The day after our conversation, she called and asked to meet me again in order to clarify a one-sided impression she might have created:

In order to be completely fair with the community, society, and with myself, I must add two more points. First, despite the pain and criticism that I expressed, I also believe that some changes have taken place. Ten years ago, at my son's *brit milah* [circumcision], the rabbi and my husband spoke and then I also rose to speak. To my dismay some people in the audience left the room and afterwards people admonished me for my *chutzpah*. "How did you dare?"

Recently, when we celebrated our daughter's *bat mitzvah,* my husband and I both spoke, and the audience was less hostile and generally more accepting. I am still basically alone, but that's another issue . . .

Secondly, I am now a board member of the synagogue—which is something new. We meet once a week, and I am one of the members who give a class on the weekly Torah portion. The men are slowly accepting the fact that they can learn something from me.

I continue fighting on every level. I feel that I can't let my guard down. When I spent a weekend with some other teachers, a rabbi spoke to us and began his address with: "Gentlemen." Afterwards, I went over to him and asked, "What about the forty percent of the audience who are women?" He actually apologized! The story about me receiving the empty book is true, but only part of the puzzle.

Even though she tries to balance the picture by coming to the defense of her community and pointing out that some changes have occurred, Bruria feels she is fighting a losing battle. Her basic perception is that, as long as she doesn't make waves, she is tolerated. At best, people have gotten used to her teaching occasionally. She participates and teaches in small informal groups where couples meet and study together. Her social impact, however, remains marginal. Even as a member of the synagogue board, she still does not have an active, public voice; only men are permitted to speak publicly within the formal context of the synagogue. At present, it is inconceivable for women to read from the Torah. In a minority of synagogues, women are permitted to deliver talks on the weekly portion, but not until the prayers are officially over.

Bruria is a deeply religious person and wants to express her religious feelings, needs, and obligations actively, in the prescribed, traditional public rituals. She has willingly accepted the obligations entailed by being a "full member" of the synagogue: she rises early and wakes her daughters for daily prayers, something traditionally only males do. Although she acknowledges differences between the sexes, she cannot tolerate situations where the differences are used to justify exclusion and silencing. The apologetic argument, as she terms it, that women are on a higher spiritual level and therefore do not require as many rituals and other religious obligations as men, she disdains as a rationalization for gender discrimination (see, for example, Meiselman 1978 or Soloveichik 1991). The general problem, Bruria is convinced, is not with Halakhah (the Jewish law) per se, but with a determination on the part of men to make the Halakhah serve a sexist ideology.

Informed of Bruria's conclusion, many of the Catholic women spoke of a distinction between the core of their religion and the way the institutions of the Church took form over the centuries. They felt that the religious establishment was a long way from Jesus and his message, especially with regard to the role of women in the Church. Lucy expressed discontent "with a male patriarchal, hierarchical Church that has emphasized what is external to us, what is not internal, that has diminished women repeatedly, that has been terrified of women." She claims that the Church has misunderstood and forgotten Jesus' true message. Seana told me that she plans to make clear to her daughter the difference between Jesus' teachings and the Church. She wants to emphasize that Catholicism is still evolving and that therefore positive change is conceivable: "I will start teaching her about my feelings of what I take issue with [in] the Catholic Church . . . I will start telling [her] the difference between the Lord's commandments and the rules of the Church—made by men, by mortals. We've altered the traditions to suit our culture at the time . . . [T]here needs to be flexibility and . . . it can be possible."

Bruria felt that the result of men's determination to make Jewish law serve a sexist agenda has been the assumption that a woman's proper place is in the home and that the synagogue is a "boys club" where men lay down the rules about how and when women may participate. Still, however deep and painful her conviction of injustice, Bruria has not considered leaving her community. It is her home, and she brings up her daughters to feel a part of it. Bruria has not seriously thought about abandoning Orthodoxy.

The Catholic women largely identified with Bruria's feelings and reasoning, but Sandra in fact did leave the Church for a while over the issue of women's participation: "It happened at my daughter's baptism that I thought this is the last time she will be able to walk on this altar until she gets married and when she dies. There is something wrong about this. So it was the last time I went to church for a very long time. I felt very strongly about it." As she told her priest, "You could be a child molester in the Catholic Church and be a priest—a criminal, but not a woman!" Her temporary solution was to become "Unitarian for a while—but I missed the Christian component very much."

Catherine, on the other hand, stayed in the Church but looked for a more progressive parish. Principally, she was disturbed at how the changes in women's education had not been followed by a concomitant change in women's participation in the rituals of the Church. Catherine knew this discontinuity firsthand:

> The universities, even some of the seminaries, have opened their doors, in terms of education classes, to women. It just stops when you get to the ritual training. And yet this course that I took on liturgy, it was taught by a nun. And she is part of a committee . . . the International Constitution of the English liturgy, something like that. It's definitely part of the hierarchy that oversees what happens ritually, in making sure everyone's following the safe guidelines and using the right tools. And here was a woman, and she teaches ritual action. She did a tremendous job. But it was very striking to think: here is someone who knows it beautifully and yet can't practice it.

Catherine was critical for a long while concerning the role of women in her parish. Long after it was common practice elsewhere, women in her parish were restricted in their participation during Mass:

> [They were] not allowed to be Eucharist ministers . . . not allowed so much as to take the empty vessels from the side table to the main altar. And I just would get very frustrated. Here I was sitting as a lector, but a man had to come and walk around to do what I was very capable of doing, and I got very frustrated with that. And so when my husband and I were dating, we decided to look for a parish that we could both become involved in . . . Women were allowed to have a much more active role. They could do the things that otherwise they just didn't do, and now with my own children, they both have become altar servers, something that I couldn't do. I think that is important.

The attitude toward women in the Catholic church has prompted Ann to feel a great distance between herself and the clergy. They cannot, she tells me, define faith for her anymore, "nor Christianity or Catholicism for that matter." She explains:

> In some ways you make do, and in other ways you thumb your nose. He—the priest—may be making stupid statements, but I am not listening . . . so you pick your battles, I guess. In other words, I won't be deprived of what I think is important . . . I think Catholic women have to be careful because, as with any of these things, if you look like you've forgotten, then it's hard to get them to move . . . If you forget, then they can move back where they were and be so stupid . . . I think it's like all the sacraments—if women are excluded, I'm not going to sacraments, but there's lots of ways of getting grace.

Ann, like Catherine, found a new place to pray—in a convent. With nuns, she feels she is respected and can express her religiosity fully. While Catherine and Ann shifted venues and Sandra took temporary refuge in the Unitarian Church, Havva and a group of like-minded Orthodox Jewish women and men decided some fifteen years ago to establish a synagogue of their own. This synagogue allows women to speak publicly about the weekly Torah portion *during* the services. In this congregation, when a girl celebrates her *bat mitzvah*, the women conduct their own service, and girls may be called to read from the Torah. At the time she was involved in establishing this synagogue, Havva believed that this kind of change was vital to her religious life and self-expression. It is interesting, however, that today she is not as convinced and single-minded as she once was. She has some doubts about the results of what she did, how and whether it reflects her current religious needs, and in particular how it affected her daughter. "Were these endeavors successful?" she now asks. "How have they developed? What consequences did they set in motion? What legacy will my children receive? Should all of these *experiments* have been done?" In other words, what has been gained and at what price? Havva now blames her daughter Tami's frustrating and painful alienation from the wider Orthodox community on "all of these experiments: They made Tami's religious world so limited."

Still, Havva wants a place in a community for herself and Tami that does not even grant "visitor visas" to women who even partially claim their voices. But what she rejected now rejects her and her daughter. She had dared hope that she lived in a religious world that would tolerate, if not welcome, various kinds of lifestyles and sensibilities, a world in which she and her daughter could express their religious feelings meaningfully and openly. As Tami gets older and more isolated from the traditional religious establishment, Havva becomes increasingly aware of the price of gaining voice. For example, she speaks of the narrow pool of liberal, young, religious men, mostly sons of her friends, who go out on dates and who would be likely to accept Tami's thinking. Her own needs and interests once constituted the framework in which Havva evaluated her decisions and actions, but now, she judges her "experiments" within the broader context of her daughter's needs and interests—hence Havva's second thoughts.

Despite her present uncertainties, though, Havva remains proud of her efforts, which she describes as an important precedent for future changes in the tradition and a message to her daughter: "You simply go out and try something, maybe because it was missing, and then you see that it was not that important. I think it [the synagogue that her group founded] is more than an institution. It is the fact that you tried, that you made an effort, that you can change something. You can create. You don't have to go along with what is. I think that is the most important lesson and message to Tami, how we *dealt with* the institutions and not the institutions themselves." That she enacted change, rather than what the change was, matters most to Havva today. Taking action—activism—is the response to oppression and silencing that she hopes her children learn from her example.

Havva and many of the other women understand that change brings with it self-doubt and feelings of loss and fear. The price of significant change within a culture—especially a religious culture where permanence and continuity are often invoked as evidence of truth—is the loss of both comfort and confirmation. Without history to count on, who can say that our way is the right way? As Rachel explains:

> With regard to the larger issue of girls' participation in synagogue life, to be quite frank, I change my opinion from morning to night and back again. Yet I really feel both things at once. Why do I have to sit behind a curtain? It's more than not having a formal role; it's this complete separation, this lack of involvement . . . But if we break with some of the tradition, then we will break with much more . . . It's possible to throw out the baby with the bath water. This is one of the answers I tell myself when I have such militant feelings. I really don't like the status quo, but I don't do anything to change it because I'm afraid of the possible consequences to the larger framework.

In contrast to Bruria's passive resentment and Havva's active initiation of change, a third response to women's exclusion from religious participation is a systematic alienation from ritual as a form of religious expression. Those who feel this alienation and defend it as a proposition may realize that there is something fundamentally wrong with women's secondary role in ritual, yet their response is a loss of interest in this facet of Jewish religious life.

Rachel, for example, sometimes holds the exact opposite of her view just quoted and quotes her sister-in-law:

> "Leave me alone. What do I care about all these men's things. Look at how great we have it! Instead of going to synagogue on Shabbat morning, we can rest in bed, read what we want . . ." I know this contradicts what I just said before, but it's the truth. Most of the time I don't really care. It makes me laugh, this "men's business"—who gets which honor in the synagogue, who gets *shlishi* [a prestigious aliyah, the honor of being called up to say a blessing over the Torah], who recites this or that blessing. It seems so childish. I feel like saying: "You guys deal with this silly business." For whatever reason, history led to this [gender] division. So be it!

I heard a similar sentiment from the Catholic women I interviewed, who quoted their daughters. Kathleen, pointing out to her daughter some of the changes that had occurred in the Church in her lifetime, emphasized that women had been prohibited from being altar servers until recently. Her daughter answered: "And now that they say we can, who says that we want to?" Whether this lack of desire came from a sense that it is too little too late, or the sense that it is "they" who have finally let "us" participate, Kathleen's daughter did not show the kind of enthusiasm she had when she was younger at the possibility of participating in church ritual on the altar.

For reasons that may be structural in origin, many Catholics did not resonate with the dilemmas that originated in the lack of participation in ritual, expressed by Kathleen or the Jewish women. Catholic women are under the same obligation as men to attend Mass weekly, to confess, and to take communion at least once a year. Jewish women are under no obligation to pray in synagogue at all.

Thus the attitude of, for instance, Elisheva is both understandable and widespread among the Jewish women interviewed:

> I respect and appreciate women who fight for their place in the synagogue. I understand that, but for me I feel no lack in the synagogue. The synagogue is a peripheral place for me. I have no connection to it. I am not interested in it. What I am willing to do and to fight for is the right to study Torah in the same way as men. Rituals, however, do not speak to me at all. Therefore, I have no problem with the status of women in the synagogue.
>
> I have a problem with formal ritual, even the rituals on Israel's Memorial and Independence Days. A good friend of mine wouldn't have a religious wedding because she wanted an egalitarian ceremony. I told her that it didn't matter because ceremonies mean nothing to me. One needs a ceremony, so be it! But what they say under the *chupah* [marriage canopy] doesn't interest me in the least. I am, in a sense, glad that I am a woman, that I am exempt from many rituals. I am not going to fight for an aliyah to the Torah or to perform some role in the synagogue. It is an area that doesn't interest me. The area of study, however, does interest me a lot.

As not only her argument but also her use of pronouns show, Elisheva believes that, as an Orthodox woman, "one" may need certain ceremonies; nevertheless, ritual is of no importance for her personally. Despite what "they" believe and are concerned about, she prefers (and here her active voice—"I"—emerges) to fight for her right to study Torah. In response to my questions, "Do you encourage your sons to take ritual seriously? Is it important for you that they attend synagogue regularly?" Elisheva answered: "It is important for me that they observe Halakhah." I persisted: "But how do you distinguish between observing Halakhah and observing the peripheral public rituals you spoke about?" She replied:

> Okay, yes . . . no! I think they have to continue observing [rituals] because they play a very serious role in the tradition. They represent

deep spiritual values. But it is not the rituals in themselves. What is important is that they [her sons] observe Halakhah.

It is very important for me that my children have a spiritual dimension in their lives. The external form that it takes is secondary. I can have a spiritual experience when I attend a good class. So if Tali decides to join a Reform synagogue because she can express herself there religiously, I will support her. It is more important for me that she goes to a Reform synagogue and has a meaningful spiritual experience than that she goes to an Orthodox synagogue and feels disgusted.

While Elisheva can find little spiritual meaning in ritual per se, she is committed to observing Halakhah; and so while she is relieved that as a woman she is exempt from having to do things that are, in any case, not traditionally part of a woman's role, she does believe that her sons must take part in synagogue services because the Halakhah requires this of men. For her, being deprived of a formal role in the synagogue is a blessing, but she would be prepared to fight for change, if the traditional attitude toward women affected her life negatively at home, in her relationships, her career, her secular life, or if women were barred from participating in religious learning. She is grateful to modern feminism for allowing a woman to become what she calls a "whole person," one who can express her full potential. But she does not consider having a public voice in religious life to be a necessary condition for being a "whole person." On the other hand, she expressed the hope that her daughter will not suffer from her mother's "muteness" but will help define "the discourse" and take part in "the discussion." Her conclusion that a "meaningful spiritual experience" matters more than its Orthodox expression struck a chord with many of the Catholic women, who said that they would not be dismayed by their daughters' choosing a different faith as long as they had a faith.

Like Elisheva, Yehudit emphasized the distinction between *talmud torah* (religious learning) and public ritual. She is very learned, in fact more so than most Orthodox men. Her school is modeled after the traditionally male *yeshivot,* and this fact has been significant in changing the traditional perception of women's learning as a private pursuit of exceptional individuals. Yehudit cites the precedent of *nashim melumadot,* women recognized for their erudition and wisdom. Though such women did not study formally in a yeshiva framework (they were often daughters of rabbis who taught them personally), Yehudit downplays the revolutionary or innovative aspects of her form of women's learning and insists "it was done before." Her attitude reflects the delicate balance between change and continuity typical of all serious attempts to enact change in a tradition. The justification of change must not only promise future benefits, but also be anchored in the past, in precedent. Yehudit looks to history for proof that the status quo is not a necessary consequence of the natural order. Although women have been generally barred in the past from studying Jewish religious texts, such study is legitimate in Yehudit's eyes because there is documented evidence of women who were acknowledged for being as learned and as scholarly as men. Still, Yehudit's studying and teaching does differ dramatically from past prototypes: learning publicly, within formal institutional settings, is a historical anomaly, and there is little doubt that she is representative of a major revolution within Orthodoxy. The hegemony of male Torah scholarship is under attack as more and more yeshivot for women are formed and as women receive stipends and support and become versed in Talmud and Midrash, in Aramaic and other traditional scholarly disciplines.

But Yehudit's total commitment to changing the status of women in the area of religious learning is not matched by a commitment on her part to women's participation in religious ritual in the synagogue. She was very clear on this point: "I have no desire to have a public role." As long, she said, as "women have a dignified place in the synagogue and I am not squeezed into a corner, I'm very happy. I'm very happy to be separate." She further claimed that, for her, *not* singing in the synagogue was a religiously significant experience: "For me, not singing allows me to feel the words and feel the song more strongly. [This is] a classic Chassidic understanding. But it really is true . . . The effort of not singing when everyone is singing generates a lot of steam. For myself, the classic Halakhic structure fits my personality pretty well."

Nevertheless, she appreciates other women's needs and desires to express themselves in the synagogue: if her daughter wanted to, Yehudit said, she would help her find a place in synagogue life. But for Yehudit to take on an active role, it would have to be in response to her daughter's need, in her capacity as a mother. Generally, Yehudit prefers to minimize the radical social significance of her *talmud torah* and instead to emphasize its intellectual significance: "It is not the fact *that* I am doing what I am doing that is new; it is rather *what* I am doing." As she sees it, what is new in her teaching is how she approaches Jewish texts. She combines her classical religious education with her general knowledge of languages, anthropology, and so forth to interpret traditional texts. Her uniqueness as a Jewish educator, she explains, resides in her ability to integrate many intellectual disciplines. For both Elisheva and Yehudit, being denied a public religious voice is not oppressive since the traditional male world of public ritual does not appeal to them. Interestingly, Yehudit remembers not always feeling this way and mentioned that when she was younger she felt that the male monopoly was unfair.

The subject of the male monopoly on ritual—on sacraments—was a topic of considerable importance for the Catholic women interviewed. Kathleen, for example, feels that women would make wonderful priests and that excluding them is unfair:

> For a long time, I was very angry about it. And I would get really ugh!
> I could feel it around the pit of my stomach . . . When my daughter
> was three years old, she had a very gregarious personality, and our pas-
> tor said to me: "You know, Mary would make a great pastor." And I

know that. I mean, that to me was almost like an ordination for her. Because it's very true about her. She's very aware of the world around her; she's very aware of people; she has a moral vision . . . That's a part of her that she'll never be able to develop in the Catholic Church . . . to the fulfillment that it deserves to be developed.

This exclusion fills her with great pain, especially when she compares her daughter to those men who are allowed to be "fulfilled" spiritually. "I'm really upset about it, very, when I see some of the people who are ordained, who don't have the same qualities. Not that I'm expecting perfection, but they're not even competent." Kathleen then goes on to list the qualities that some priests do not have—whereas her daughter and other women she knows who are denied the possibility of ordination do. Many priests, she says, "can't preach, don't have a sense of place, don't have the heart for justice, don't have the kind of hunger that I've seen in Mary and other women."

Kathleen describes this as "a part of the church that's really wounded," and she confides that her whole commitment to and role in the Church are sometimes undermined when she considers its gender bias: "I sit there at prayer on Sundays, and I think sometimes: 'Why do I do this to myself? Why am I here?'" She tried to mitigate the gender bias of the Catholic tradition in her own classroom by "ritualizing" activities that were "more inclusive" and by looking for aspects of the tradition that include women. But "you know," she added emphatically, "you still come up against the wall, all the time, all the time. And I worked so hard." Still, Kathleen framed the limitations and problems of her religion within a larger context of human limits. "The world is not perfect," she said, "so why should I expect a human institution [to be]? Even if we believe it was instituted by God, it's still filled with human beings. It cannot be perfect. However, I can work to do whatever I can to make it a little better. Or at least I can ask questions. See, I think that's my ministry . . . to ask questions. I don't know if anyone will ever get the answers, but as long as I ask the question, somebody has to think about it."

Sandra sees progress, but not enough. She acknowledges that there have been changes in the Church from when she was a girl, when her mother used to do all the work for the altar before the services but when only a male would be allowed to place the Eucharistic elements (bread and wine) there. Today, Sandra's daughter is an altar girl: "My daughter decided to become an altar girl. She and her friend are the first girls in the history of this parish. It is a job that was not open to girls when I was a child, *but it still ain't the priesthood.*" As long as women are not ordained, she believes, gender discrimination is inherent, whatever other progress has been made: "I still feel a lot of discomfort . . . I go through waves, and when I read when they reaffirm that women can't be priests, I get really angry. I have strong feelings about this subject." Despite leaving the Church for a while on this account and looking into other Christian churches, she returned to the Catholic Church, resigned to bringing her daughter up in a less than perfect situation but one that is slowly changing. "I hope," she adds, that "this generation of girls can save the Church."

Ann agrees: "I sat in classes with men who were going to be priests, and they were so stupid . . . It was enough to know that we can't beat it. You can't make them [change]. You have to keep living your life against them." For Ann the fact that women are not ordained is not simply a problem for Catholic women: "The patriarchy has made the norm and women's roles, but *they* are losing out; we *all* are."

Jacqueline was more ambivalent. She commented on how many roles are now open to women that once were closed, and she herself has played them: "I'm a Eucharist minister. I distribute communion. I preach, because lots of times a priest won't show up who's supposed to be there. I had a May procession one time," but here her narrative grows more negative: "I had two priests sitting over in the rectory. I was so annoyed that they didn't want to come over. They didn't show up." Jacqueline told me that she, in any case, enjoys what she does in the church, and while upset that the priests will not attend when she stands in for them, feels their life is not terribly enviable: "I think their life is extremely difficult. It's very unnatural. Yes, I would love to say Mass. I wouldn't want to do the rest of it. I don't even think I would like living in a community the way, say, a Jesuit does. I wouldn't want to give away any more of my life than I already do to my school." Although theoretically Jean spoke of gender discrimination, the hardships priests endure do not make that calling terribly attractive to her, hence her conclusion that "I'm very comfortable with my role today."

Many of the women, Jewish and Catholic alike, had moved from indignation to acceptance; some, like Yehudit, have come to find beauty in silence. A psychological analysis of their expressed preferences might invoke a standard "defense mechanism" explanation: people cease to desire what is believed to be unattainable. Viewing participation in ritual life as a burden or as less than all-important is not necessarily a sign of bad faith or of unconscious rationalization—though, doubtless, some of the religious women I interviewed would find it to be so.

Daughters and Sons

"I would not feel terrible if my children would not be religious when they grow up. Actually, it would be harder for me if Uri, my son, were to stop being religious." These were Sima's opening remarks in our conversation dealing with her differing expectations of her son and daughters. We talked about the effects of traditional cultural idioms of masculinity and femininity on mothering:

> When my son was born, I had the feeling "now I am contributing something significant to society." I was very uncomfortable with these feelings, but they were really there. I was embarrassed that alongside my cognitive views [of gender equality], I had this gut reaction to my

son. And I still have very different expectations of him because he is a son.

I feel that he has a special claim to intellectual development. If he were not to learn how to study Talmud on a high level, I would feel truly awful. I would feel that it was a terrible betrayal of tradition, of my roots, of my father and grandfather. Of course, I also want the girls to become well versed in Talmud, but it does not have the same emotional importance. For me, being learned is a sign of manhood [embarrassed giggle]. Just as going to the army and becoming an officer are tests of masculinity for certain families in Israel, for me it is studying Talmud (even if he decides to have a career in the "normal" world).

Sima distinguishes between her own "cognitive" commitments and her inner, visceral commitment to her son's place in the chain of Jewish history. Her father is a learned and distinguished head of a well-known yeshiva. She feels intuitively connected to this dynasty through her son and sees her daughters as having a more tangential relation to it: "I feel that he has to continue the tradition, but the girls are more freed of this yoke."

Rachel is uneasy about similar feelings since they contradict what she would like to believe:

In spite of the atmosphere of equality that is around these days and which reflects what I think, I still feel that learning Torah is a value particularly for boys. It sounds absurd to say this because it is not a biological distinction. Yet it feels almost like a biological distinction, like, women get pregnant and have babies, while men . . . I know the comparison is ridiculous because one is biological and the other is social. Still, I can't help seeing it almost as a biological difference.

I don't want the girls to be completely ignorant of parts of their cultural heritage, but I expect from them basically what I expect of secular Jews, that is, familiarity with the texts. I expect much more from my son and from boys in general. I just don't feel the same need for my daughters. Maybe it's because of what I am used to; maybe there is a contradiction in me. I expect them [the girls] to get an equal secular education. I don't completely reject the idea that my daughter will become very learned in Judaica . . . but it is not *that* important for me.

Neither Rachel nor Sima can escape the powerful influence of traditional definitions of gender difference. For them, the defining characteristic of masculinity is not an aptitude for Little League baseball or the ethos of the Israeli Army, but being knowledgeable in the Talmud. Although each feels free to question the authority of her tradition, neither is free of the psychological authority of its cultural symbols of masculinity and femininity. Shoshi grew up with these same gender expectations, but in her case the sense of exclusion was more pronounced. It was gender alone that explained her brother's exclusive right to study Talmud:

When I was in grade four, my brother started to study Talmud. I felt completely frustrated. I remember sitting next to him and my father, trying to catch on to what they were learning but to no avail. I was never included. This feeling became even more acute when the boys in our elementary school went to yeshiva high schools, and the system of segregated [by sex] education began. The boys studied Judaica on a very high level, and we were not given the same opportunities. I felt that I would never be able to catch up. Even when I started to study, I always had this basic feeling of frustration, that I would never really catch up.

Shoshi is grateful today that she and her daughter can study. When her daughter was a little girl, she tried to compensate for the gender bias she herself had experienced as a girl by emphasizing the lighting of candles on Friday night (traditionally done by women) as a major event. She wanted her daughter to feel that there was something positive and important for girls in the tradition. When her son asked to light candles together with them, she answered: "Sorry. This is something special for girls."

On Celebrating a Daughter's Bat Mitzvah

Feelings of indignation or anger and a sense of injustice that adolescent girls often feel as a result of gender biases are often relived when women find themselves in the role of teachers guiding their daughters through adolescence. Mothers may have an opportunity to preserve their daughters' voices, and to jar their own memories as well. I therefore asked the Jewish women I interviewed how they prepared their daughters for their *bat mitzvahs,* for the rite of passage into adulthood. How did their own memories and desires for the future affect their expectations for their daughters? What in Jewish tradition did they want to preserve, and what did they want to modify? The *bat mitzvah,* being a modern innovation, is more open to modification and forms of self-expression than other rituals. How did these mothers prepare and celebrate?

Rachel's daughters' *bat mitzvahs* were celebrated with parties at home, while her son's *bar mitzvah* celebration took place in a banquet hall. When reflecting on this and other differences, Rachel could not help but acknowledge the obvious injustice of this traditional form of discrimination between sons and daughters: "Externally there was a big difference between the parties for my son and for my daughters. It may appear to be merely technical, but it is more than that. I now feel that it was not right, and I ask myself, why did we not do more for the girls? Also, I did not deal with the larger issues about what it means to be a woman, what changes you are about to go through. In their schools, they had classes about who they identify with, etc., but I didn't speak to them about that at all."

In contrast to Rachel's lack of personal communication with her daughters, Miriam remembers having had "significant" conversations with her daughter around *bat mitzvah* time:

> Beforehand, it was just regular mother-daughter stuff like, "How was your day?" "Go clean up your room." But as her *bat mitzvah* approached,

things became more significant [Miriam used this adjective also to describe her present relationship with her daughter]. We started studying about different women in history. I thought it would be really important for her to know more about women, to have different role models. But when she asked me, "Mother, why is it so important for you to teach me about these women?" I was really shocked to realize that she wasn't aware of the problem of being a woman and a mother. I was sure that she had been aware of my conflicts with being a woman and a mother, of trying to do different things.

There was a point in our learning—when we studied about Dvorah the prophetess—that really shook me up. She made the point that from the biblical text we don't know whether Dvorah was married. Then she added: "Mom, you can't do it all in life. It [the text] doesn't say whether she was a mother." I thought to myself: "Is Dvorah really a role model?" She had pinpointed the problem for me. I also began thinking about whether my daughter suffered because of my life choices.

The women whom Miriam and her daughter discussed in preparation for the *bat mitzvah* were all exceptional women whom history deemed worthy to recall and who could serve as significant role models. But the result of these study sessions turned out to be a lesson for Miriam: the female types that she thought would surely impress her daughter failed to do so, and, as a consequence of her daughter's critique, Miriam began to question some of her own assumptions. Miriam's recollection of this incident came in the midst of a conversation about being a religious woman in the twentieth century: "My identity is made up of the fact that I am a woman, a religious person, a mother, a career person, . . . someone who lives in the twentieth century. There is a conflict between these different aspects, and I feel this conflict all the time."

Asked how she deals with these conflicts, she recalled her response to her daughter's *bat mitzvah:*

When we were young, we thought about how to solve the problem [of women's participation in religious ritual]. But the problem remained.

Now we think about how much time and energy to devote to certain things without resolving the problem. Take, for example, my daughter's *bat mitzvah*. I could have stood on my head and gone crazy, wagged my tail and carried on about how women should have a role in the synagogue and about how much they have to offer. The energy and emotion I would have had to put forth would have been lost on my daughter who anyway does not share my pathos and convictions on this matter. So, I had to compromise with reality. So, we did what we did, and we celebrated how we celebrated, which was suitable for my daughter. And we all felt happy, some of us more, some of us less.

Miriam described herself as a woman who often succumbs to the dictates of her community and, in our interview, was critical of her own feelings and passivity. "Maybe it's a sign that it doesn't really bother me enough," she confessed after describing her daughter's relatively conventional *bat mitzvah* celebration. Miriam's caricature of herself standing upside down and "wagging her tail" in order to get her convictions across to her daughter or to her community is a revealing self-parody that reflects how women may view themselves in the light of the hysterical-woman stereotype. A woman who expresses herself forcefully and emotionally is often not seen as a person seeking her own voice or expressing a legitimate wish for self-actualization or trying to educate her daughter about the value of living an active religious life, but rather as a loud, raucous, and basically infantile female.

Miriam was not willing to appear ridiculous, especially given that her chances of success were negligible. She knew that her own need for a religious voice was not a need her daughter shared. It is interesting that in many areas of their daughters' upbringing these mothers felt no qualms about enforcing their own agenda and did not feel the need to reflect what their daughters really wanted, while in the case of the *bat mitzvah,* they were reluctant to press the issue with their daughters unless the girls themselves expressed the need.

The disparity between what daughters and mothers expected from a *bat mitzvah* was most pronounced in the case of Sara. Sara had taken a sabbatical and moved her whole family to a smaller community in order to spend the year of her daughter's *bat mitzvah* in a more meaningful way. There was an Orthodox synagogue there where women could take part in the services. It soon became apparent, however, that the pressing need to celebrate her daughter's *bat mitzvah* in this way was more Sara's than her daughter's. At first, Sara felt hurt, disappointed, and resentful. How could her daughter—the daughter of one of the most celebrated religious feminists in the country, a woman who had fought publicly for women's religious rights and equality—not want to read from the Torah in the synagogue and thus celebrate her coming of age as boys do? In time, however, Sara came to accept that these were her own needs, not her daughter's:

> I realize that what happened this year concerning her *bat mitzvah* was idiotic. *I* wanted to learn to read from the Torah, so I wanted my daughter to have a *bat mitzvah for me* in the synagogue. Why should she want this? What can I do? She just doesn't want it!
>
> But it hurts me very much, and I feel disappointed. I had a dream, and it didn't work out. She said "no" to my sense of self, to my self-image as a mother, to my worldview. She wants to decide for herself. It could be that in the end she will reach the same conclusions as I did, but she has to go through the process on her own.

Still, her daughter's rejection had far-reaching implications for Sara and for their relationship. Her daughter felt unable to live in the same house as Sara and, soon after their arrival in Tel Aviv, returned home to Nevei Galim. It was only after this separation and their subsequent reconciliation that they could live together—as mother and daughter, not ideological adversaries. Some mothers seem aware from the start that their daughters may not share their own attitudes toward ritual. For example, Shoshi, when I asked if she encourages her daughter to participate in formal rituals from which women and girls are generally excluded, answered:

> I don't, and the reason is because I am afraid she will see me as a kind of feminist mother and she will be tempted to run in the opposite direction. I have a neighbor who carries the banner of equality all the time. She goes to synagogue on Succoth with *lulav* and *etrog* in hand [the ritual of carrying four species of plant on this festival], and her daughter is embarrassed by this.
>
> I try to keep a low profile in this area so that she will not become antagonistic . . . but if she were to come to me and ask me to teach her *taame' hamikrah* [scriptural music notations], I would certainly help and encourage her.

"I encourage her to study," Shoshi says of her daughter's intellectual religious development, but she takes a hands-off position toward ritual, allowing her daughter to define the rules for herself. Shoshi is cautious even about telling her daughter her own views, which demand "religious fulfillment in formal rituals" for women. She has chosen instead to wait and see how her daughter will come to express her own needs.

Yehudit likewise made a point of listening to her daughter's needs and interests when planning her *bat mitzvah*:

> We did a particular project together and celebrated the *bat mitzvah* in our house. I invited a number of friends. There was music, a little singing, and a few speeches, by women mostly. I don't know whether it was a spiritual high point. It was just a very pleasant, thoughtful, and warm experience. I don't know . . . Boys' *bar mitzvahs* are so much more of a spiritual experience . . . If I felt her moving towards something, looking for something else, I would try to go with her. All those big things just don't suit me, but if she had been that type, I would have compromised on it.

A theme expressed in virtually all of these interviews is that girls ought to be allowed to decide the scope and content of their own *bat mitzvah* celebrations. One might have expected, therefore, to hear about one daring experiment after another. But, the girls had been brought up in religious communities and did not want to "stand out," to deviate from the standard norms of their social milieus. They felt no real need to break the male hegemony on public ritual practices or to challenge the traditional boundaries separating men and women in the synagogue. Either they lacked their mothers' awareness of and concern with "the problem" or they simply succumbed to the more powerful social and peer pressures to conform. Moreover, the mothers' feminist idealism was also tempered by social and interpersonal considerations.

Although the issue of religious participation was pressing for only some of the women, all believed that the status quo could be changed without destroying the tradition. Most said that if their daughters were to show an interest in greater religious participation (a situation they could envision), they would respond positively and help them realize their goals. In this respect, these women differed from their own mothers, who would have justified the exclusion of women as a given and unalterable characteristic of Jewish religious life and practice.

Most of the women in the group I interviewed seemed poised to struggle for change but needed an impetus from and the support of their daughters before they could move toward activism. Mothering could bring them to feel justified and empowered in bringing about change. It would appear that the selfless role of mother is ironically the role in which these religious women were most ready to press for reforms that would improve their own and their daughters' personal and communal lives. As women, they would tolerate the situation even if it was not "right," but as mothers, if their daughters experienced pain, they could and would make sure "a way would be found."

Without an established community to support and legitimate gender-related change, these women continue to struggle with "the problem" and with the ambiguity of their multiple commitments. Allowing their daughters the option of celebrating their *bat mitzvahs* like all the other girls freed the women from having to "stand on their heads" and "wag their tails" like a "feminist mother" who "carries the banner of equality all the time." They did not want to "make an issue" of their daughters' initiation into adulthood. Whatever the underlying reasons—the fear of socially isolating their daughters, the desire to avoid schisms within the family, their personal feelings of alienation and lack of interest in ritual observances—these liberated Orthodox women went along with the existing norms of their communities, leaving the final battle to raise women's voices in the synagogue for later generations.

A Unique Institution

The parallel to *bat mitzvah* in the life of a Catholic girl might be confirmation. Catholic boys are confirmed too, just as boys have *bar mitzvahs,* but in the Catholic Church, there is no distinction between the confirmation ceremonies of boys and girls, and indeed they are confirmed together. Perhaps because of this equivalence, confirmation was not brought up ever as a problem, but rather as an example of the last time the girls and boys could be equal.

In the Roman Catholic Church, besides the priesthood and the monastic world, there is also the world of women religious, that is, of nuns. Nuns, like priests and monks, isolate themselves to some degree from daily secular life; all take vows of "poverty, chastity, and obedience." Each must have a demonstrated vocation before taking vows. All devote their lives to the Church, to social work, to education, and to their own and others' spiritual growth and religious commitment. Although not the equal of priests in the Church hierarchy, nuns have a very special status—parallel, one might say, to the status of the Virgin Mary—that has absolutely no counterpart in the Jewish world.

A plethora of material about nuns, based on new historical research, has emerged in recent years, and the work especially of feminist historians has undermined the stereotypes. Many of the women religious appeared to have chosen a cloistered life in order to free themselves from the burden of marriage to a husband not of their choosing and to be able to devote their lives to their personal development. Often nuns could move about more freely than other women in their time and could acquire an education. They could spend their days in the company of women, of often like-minded friends, and sometimes in joint artistic pursuits (the illumination of manuscripts, for example). These studies point to a less conventional and more complex "class" of women, one more attractive to the modern sensibility.[1]

Many of the Catholic women I interviewed discussed the institution of nuns and spoke often of specific women they knew who were nuns. Perhaps out of fascination with what was for me a novel subject, a world of women beyond my experience as a Jew, I asked them to elaborate on their relationship to women religious. For the women interviewed, the institution of the convent embodied, on the one hand, the most traditional role for Catholic women and the least rewarded or honored and, on the other hand, a role that brought with it much prestige, even a fair amount of power within the Church hierarchy. The women's ambivalence perhaps reflected the actual complexities of the institution itself. Mother Teresa's power was formidable, but most women religious obviously never attain that kind of stature, and when compared to the power of the male priests, the lesser power of nuns seemed to the women I interviewed a poor acknowledgment of their sacrifice. They said that the nuns' vocation was generally treated as a lower form of religiosity.

In particular, Sandra thought that the nuns represented a class of women doing "the lesser jobs" in the Church and said that this fact had a detrimental effect on the development of strong and independent women in the Catholic faith. Not only did she feel badly for the nuns themselves, but she also felt that the very existence of such a "class" affected the way Catholic girls are brought up and represented the ideal type held up by the Catholic Church for emulation by women. That there are fewer nuns now than in the past seemed a positive development for her, since the decline has lessened the effect of a submissive role model for women. It was not that Sandra did not appreciate some of what nuns undertake and accomplish, but she was more keenly conscious of their negative influence as role models. When lay women participate during Mass, she said, they tend frequently to wear that "holy Mary look": "There is a feeling . . . that women are supposed to be serene, perfect, ever-serving creatures. I think you get it less nowadays, 'cause you don't have so many nuns doing the lesser jobs."

Kathleen taught in schools with nuns as colleagues and so had daily interactions with them. She experienced them as having considerable power in those schools, though she realized that part of their power came from how hard they worked. Often, Kathleen told me, a nun would be chosen to be principal over one of the lay teachers: "If you could choose between two, choose the sister, because, well, first of all, she could give you 90 hours a day without anybody ever saying, 'Aren't you ever coming home?'" Kathleen expressed deep feelings about the injustice of the sisters' work not being truly respected and classed with that of priests, about the injustice of lacking "the power of being able to name" their work. She said of the nuns' service "that what you do is truly the same kind of work that someone who's ordained is doing in many ways, but it is not honored in the same way at all."

Kathleen felt that many young women today who feel a religious calling are finding other avenues to express themselves. A friend of her daughter's, for example, "chose a theology degree and works as an advocate for poor and homeless people in San Francisco, rather than join a religious order." Nonetheless, Kathleen maintains a deep respect for nuns herself: "Women religious have been doing incredible work over the years, really, really." She positions herself differently from most people with regard to the hardships of nuns: "Many women see religious life as another controlling thing. They don't see it as freedom, which really it is for so many women. Freedom to be celibate, freedom to study, a freedom to work as you choose, a freedom to be with other women in community and not to have to be concerned about their sexuality."

The more prevalent sentiment was that women religious sacrifice much, for little in return. Marianne told me: "We're very close to several nuns, older nuns now, and I look at them and think of how much of their life they gave up and they really don't have a life. Their lifestyle, in their late eighties, is really sad. It's like almost poverty. It's not like that with the respect that some of the priests had, [and the nuns] gave up just as much, if not more."

Catherine said likewise and with bitterness: "When you think how our nuns are viewed—they give up their lives, just the same as a priest, the same idea of marrying the church—and yet they have no status in the church whatsoever. It is the nuns who began this move for women to be involved and doing more." Jacqueline has profited from the move to involve women, and she contrasted her "good fortune" with the fate of the nuns. She felt that as a laywoman, as a teacher, as a female religious scholar, she has been able to incorporate much more into her life than the nuns can. She recalls once meeting a very intelligent sister: "She believed that she was going to be the first woman priest. She was very excited about that, and yet she never got to do it. But I think in maybe that setting—where you're extremely educated, where your whole life is dedicated to that—. . . women in a community very often feel that way. Many sisters I know feel very repressed, and they are. I'm not; I have it all. They don't."

Despite all of this candid concern about the fate of women religious, some of the Catholic mothers I spoke with said that, if their daughters decided to take vows, they would encourage or at least not discourage them, since the nun's way of life, the religious calling of nuns, seemed to them in certain ways positive.

The Catholic mothers' ambivalence toward this unique aspect of their religion—despite the immensity of difference between Catholic and Jewish institutions in the expression of women's religiosity—was matched by the Jewish mothers' ambivalence toward their daughters' acquiescence to the community's religious norms and toward their own role of observer rather than participant in synagogue. What these Jewish and Catholic women share is not a set of institutions, but their ambivalence toward aspects of their religious institutions.

CHAPTER THREE

Abdications and Coalitions

There are times when ambiguity is more indicative of normality than of abnormality. The current situation of women in Western society is a good example of this. If this observation holds for Western women, in general, then it certainly holds for women who are religious, particularly for those with secular educations and modern expectations. The boundaries between competing social ideals have been eroded and blurred, so that the availability of alternative ways of life as "live options" has made radical ambiguity a common feature of ordinary social experience.

Given this situation, it would be superfluous for me to conclude that the modern yet religious women I interviewed felt ambivalence and ambiguity in their combined roles of mother and cultural agent. The absence of perceived ambiguity would require more explanation than its presence. These interviews did not reveal *that* the women were conflicted but rather showed *how* they experienced and managed the conflicts they faced.

In raising their daughters, religious women are socializers with responsibility to the community and allegiance to an orthodoxy. But, they also experience their relationships with their daughters in ways that transcend their social contexts. The socializing role is complicated by the fact that the community's notion of socialization is sometimes at odds with what these women hope to achieve. The community expects conformity to its religious standards, while this group of mothers would like to see their daughters eventually walk the same fine line they walk—that is, resist the roles that normative religion assigns to women, but without abandoning the system.

The result of this ambivalence is that women often speak to their daughters in two distinct voices: one that conveys weakness and doubt, and one that expresses strength and clarity. The latter, they tend to believe, can be dangerous to their daughters and to their tradition, and, therefore, they more often use the former, fully realizing the possible negative consequences this choice might have on their daughters, themselves, and their relationships.

The women stand, though sometimes tentatively, with both feet in tradition, so even as they challenge the ideas or assumptions behind normative prescriptions of behavior, they, by and large, comply with those norms. In their relationships with their daughters and in their roles as agents of socialization, the women face two questions of opposite tendency: first, at what point does resistance turn into rebellion? and, second, at what point does compliance silence their independent inner voices? They want to bequeath to their daughters a stance of resistance *within* tradition, an ambivalent conformity that does not negate their daughters' individuality—does not negate their inner world. In the final analysis, their allegiance to religious authority is such that they may be willing to muffle their own inner voice so as to ensure their daughters' loyalty to theirs.

Few will risk preaching a resistance that could lead their daughters into open rebellion against traditional values. Still, they believe (or want to believe) that the voice that says, "Don't make waves; Fit in," is less influential than the voice that insists, "Explore your uniqueness." Yet, because they do not feel secure in their unconventional attitude toward religion, and because they are not certain they can pass it on to the next generation, the voice of conformity is heard all too clearly by their daughters.

Some of the women wonder whether their own questions and reservations about their religion are suitable only for adults—for mature individuals who are deeply committed to the system and sufficiently stable and established to dare question it. As a result, some tend to choose relatively conservative schools for their daughters and relatively conventional communities in which to raise them. Ironically, the women are disappointed when those social and educational institutions prove successful and are disconcerted by their daughters' complacency, conformity, and lack of autonomy. They hope that eventually their daughters will learn to appreciate the need for cultural resistance. After all, their daughters are repeating the same educational process they themselves underwent—a formal education that assures allegiance, together with an exposure to ideas that promote questions and challenges.

After much deliberation, Yehudit decided to send her daughter to a school that was educationally more rigid and more religiously conservative than any school she herself would be willing to attend:

> I chose to send her to Ulpana because I was afraid that religiously the other schools would not be positive enough. Ulpana encourages *yirat shamayim* [reverence of God]. I felt my own weakness in making clear statements about these things at home. I find it hard to talk about *yirat shamayim,* so I felt I wanted the school to do that for me. I wanted her to get something clear from her peer group, straight answers: "yes" or "no." There are doubts in my mind whether it was the right decision.

Yehudit's choices were characterized by a lack of enthusiasm and self-confidence. She felt that ambiguity, vagueness, and complexity generally reflect the nature of living with respect to her religious community (as she said in other parts of the interview). With respect to her daughter's religious education, she viewed clarity and decisiveness as virtues and the inability to make simple yes/no judgments as a vice. Fear of God, she felt, must be conveyed in straightforward, didactic discourse.

Once the school that Yehudit had chosen showed signs of success on its own terms, she became dissatisfied. She and her husband developed "a slightly adversarial relationship to her school":

> The teacher seems to be pushing a position . . . [while] I would like to see a much more open attitude. For instance, she is subtly indicating that she is not in favor of national service, which is a surprise to me. She is not saying it blatantly but more like: "If you meet someone wonderful, you should not close your minds to it [marriage]." It is part of her agenda to get them onto the straight path, away from danger, because all kinds of things could happen. I don't want to do her teacher injustice, but Adina knows what my attitude is.

Yehudit is critical of Adina's teacher for conveying messages about the dangers of the outside world. Adina's teacher seems to believe that the best way to protect girls is to get them married immediately after high school—a view that Yehudit opposes. Yehudit believes that Adina is aware of her opposition but doubts whether she can succeed in convincing her daughter. "I probably did not succeed," she concludes: "I have a question about the religious part [of Adina's schooling]. I am not sure I managed to communicate that to her very well. I don't know what she gets from it. That is where I don't feel I've managed to communicate with her, to balance things."

Yehudit chose a school that she thought would supply her daughter with inner balance. The school she chose could not do so precisely because of its unambiguous religious outlook, the educational philosophy that Yehudit thought would do Adina good. Balance and harmony are not parts of the school's educational agenda.

Yehudit's expressions of doubt contrast with what she sees as her daughter's no-nonsense attitude toward religion.[1] Yehudit's comments about Adina's education conclude as follows: "I feel that I am constantly struggling. For example, what do you feel religiously when a friend dies? I found I was very involved in such a situation. She [Adina] would not even ask questions like that, which means I probably did not succeed. She would never ask, how could God do that? She is her own person. Very much so. She has, in a way, a very conventional attitude [toward] religion."

When I asked Yehudit whether her wanting Adina to remain an Orthodox Jew has prevented their discussing some of the complexities of being religious, she answered that the opposite was in fact the case: "The things that I tend to share with her are the complexities of my thinking about the world, the kinds of things that can be talked about [secular topics]. I am afraid I might have overdone it."

As we have seen, Yehudit divides the universe of discourse she shares with her daughter into what can be talked about—secular topics that do not require hard-and-fast answers—and religious issues, which, while complex in the adult world, only require a yes-or-no response for a child or teenager. Along with her fears that her daughter does not know or appreciate her religious complexity, she is also anxious about the harmful effect of the "complex views" she sometimes airs at home.

Rachel likewise chose a disciplined, right-wing, all-girls school for her daughters, though she taught in a more liberal institution where she enjoyed greater openness and freedom. She rationalized her decision to teach in a more liberal school as a personal preference. "I teach in Bet Sarah for my soul," she said, the implication being that what was good for *her* soul might not be good for *her daughters'* souls—in fact, it might be detrimental. Her daughters' school "directs the girls in one direction. There is no ambiguity. I think there is a big difference between what adolescents can handle and what adults need. I teach at Bet Sarah. It is important for me, but I do not think that adolescents have to be exposed to all those questions. I tell parents thinking about sending their children to this school, Bet Sarah, that it is a gamble. They can win, but, if they lose, they will lose much more than they would at another school. I chose not to take that gamble with my girls."

While choosing any educational institution involves risks, the dangers are not always equivalent. At one school, openness may lead to heterodoxy and disloyalty to tradition, while at another, narrowness may inhibit a girl from developing all aspects of herself. The conflict at times comes down to loyalty to tradition or loyalty to the self. Rachel is thus keenly aware of the possible consequences of her choosing a conventional but safe schooling for her daughters, yet she is less than completely satisfied with her decision:

> It is hard for me to think of my daughter choosing a male kind of career where she would have to invest so much of herself and would be considered a threat to certain men. I think she presents herself with expectations that are realistic and she conforms with the norms of her peers. I have ambivalent feelings about that. On the one hand, it bothers me that she won't develop herself; on the other hand, I understand her. I think she would be willing to conform, to sacrifice herself in order to fit in with her husband's needs.

Rachel believes that the price of her daughters' conformity to peer groups will ultimately be self-denial in the name of satisfying a husband's social needs. To be in relationship with men is to appease men, to give up part of yourself in order not to threaten a potential husband's ego. Rachel is unhappy about the prospective human cost of the schooling she has chosen for her girls. They will probably live according to a script that will keep parts of them submerged. Yet, at the same time, she understands this choice and may even see it as necessary.

Education—and especially religious education—involves more than intellectual development—of this Rachel and Yehudit remain acutely conscious. Yehudit points to the lack of religious depth and sensitivity in the school she chose. She points to the absence of those religious dimensions she most appreciates and values. Rachel focuses more on personal development, on the obsessive concern of her daughters' peers with becoming a "good wife."

Neither Yehudit nor Rachel attempts to whitewash the negative effects of the choice of schools on their daughters, or to downplay the significance of these institutions as compared with their influence as mothers and role models. Now, each woman stoically accepts the consequences of her choice as unavoidable, or at least as preferable to the alternatives.

In any event, their choice of schools had indirect benefits for the mothers themselves. Sending her daughters to an uncompromisingly Orthodox school gave Rachel the freedom and license to continue to be a more liberal parent: "I am in an easy position. I can be the understanding one, the more lenient one, compared to what their school demands of them. It is much easier and more pleasant to be an open, liberal parent than to be a strict one."

By sending her daughters to Lustig, which has a "very strict dress code," for example, Rachel could continue to be an "understanding," "lenient," "pleasant," "liberal," and "easy" parent straight through the difficult years of adolescence. Her daughters' school relieved her of the onus of socializing them into the religious discipline of Judaism. Despite this sense of relief and liberation regarding matters of discipline, however, Rachel clearly feels that she is not free to voice her opinions, often negative, about the religious establishment. For instance, she is very critical of the place assigned to women in Judaism, and she does not accept rabbinical hegemony; yet, she questions whether and to what extent to share her strong views with her daughters.

Rachel is afraid of leading her daughters astray, but she also believes that they somehow know her opinions even without her expressing them. She is so absorbed in her own convictions that she is convinced everyone around her must be aware of them:

> With regard to feminist issues in the home, about sharing the workload, etc., I don't tell them about it explicitly, but I think I really tell them because they know where I stand. The same is true with religious and political issues. They can't grow up in our home without knowing some of my quandaries. My relatives always take what the rabbis say at face value. I don't feel that way, but I don't feel I have to share that with them all the time. They will be exposed to the world of questions when they are older, at the university.
>
> I would not say out loud that I do not think that the Halakhah can solve every problem . . . I also now try to be more quiet at home, for example, not to argue with my father-in-law about feminist things. One doesn't have to say everything that's on one's mind.
>
> My daughters tell me to stop fighting with the world—not because they don't agree with me but because they want more peace at home. I am not one hundred percent sure they actually agree with me, though.

Rachel feels she may have the luxury of silence because a part of her believes she has conveyed her beliefs and disbeliefs nonverbally. Her silence apparently is so loud that her daughters must surely have heard even what was not said. In the end, however, Rachel realizes that her daughters do not necessarily share her views. She accepts the fact that her religious voice may have been muffled by louder voices competing for her daughters' attention.

Miriam left city life in Jerusalem for the homogeneity of a religious settlement, but was concerned, like Yehudit and Rachel, by her daughter's successful socialization in this environment: "I am disappointed that she always listens to her friends. The group is the most important thing for her. She will do things just because they do them. Because of her personality, I think she will fit into what is accepted in our community. She is not a fighter. She accepts the norm. She does what everyone else does. 'This is what everyone does' is her favorite expression."

Miriam is less understanding of her daughter Merav's conformity than Rachel is of her daughters'. She wants Merav to evince the spirit of autonomy she was taught at home. The justification, "This is what everyone does," should not have crossed her daughter's mind, Miriam believes. Although, after expressing disappointment with Merav's conformity, Miriam corrected herself for creating a one-sided impression and for slighting individualistic aspects of her daughter's behavior. "When she goes to class," Miriam noted, "she sometimes expresses her father's or mother's unconventional opinions. But," she continued, "I do not think that feminist issues are really issues for her. When I was her age, I already had thought about and was bothered by these things, but she is not at all."

Sometimes, however, Merav is a good daughter in Miriam's opinion, for example, when she "comes home from school and tells me that I would be proud of her because she expressed a feminist opinion which was not the norm." Of course, these unconventional attitudes are Miriam's, not Merav's. Even when she gives voice to "correct" opinions, Merav is not really expressing herself, her own opinions. She knows that her parents hold unconventional views, and she sometimes expresses them herself, but basically this is another act of conformity. The community voice is by far the most influential voice for Merav, it is the voice she regards as her own. That voice is powerful in shaping even Miriam's choices and way of life. While she prides herself on her independence and individuality, Miriam knows that she is neither "a loner" nor an iconoclast untouched by "what everyone does": "I feel that we stand alone in our community on political issues and that is difficult for her [Merav].

She was so relieved when I told her that Mr. X also voted as we did. We do not have a VCR in our home, but, in the end, we are *quite similar to most of the people who live here.*"

Sara's disappointment with her daughter's behavior centers primarily on religious issues. Her daughter Hadas failed to internalize Sara's values and has chosen a more right-wing, ultrareligious life than her mother's. Once again, the crosscurrents of wanting and not wanting one's daughter to "be like them" inform Sara's analysis of Hadas's religious identity.

- *Current A: Be like them; be a good girl:* "I want her to be not only like me but better than me. I want her to be everything that I am not. I want her to be properly religious, with the correct opinions, get married at the right time, in other words, earlier than I did."

- *Current B: Why are you like them (and not like me)?* "When she said 'no' to this kind of *bat mitzvah,* she said 'no' to me, but on second thought . . ."

- *Transition before returning to Current B:* ". . . it is her right. She is quite ultra-Orthodox in terms of the way she dresses. My husband and I both went through an ultra-Orthodox period before reaching a synthesis in our lives."

- *Current A: I understand why you prefer to be like them rather than like me:* "I understand her allergy to the quasi-traditional type of modern Orthodoxy. It also drives me crazy, even though I am less strictly observant than my daughter. I can't stand the laxness that hides behind slogans of religious openness. It's baloney. It's not openness. It's not serious. I am very proud that in my family it is more real and more serious. It is natural that at her age she takes the whole business more seriously."

Sara's ambivalence is obvious. In many parts of the interview, she expresses considerable dismay over her daughter's religious choices that are different from her own. Yet, she not only understands but also congratulates her daughter for her seriousness and earnestness. Hadas goes so far as to question openness as a form of hypocrisy. Unlike Rachel's daughters wanting only domestic peace and Miriam's daughter opting for conformity, Hadas is in Sara's eyes a nonconformist and rebel in her own right, despite her rejection of her mother's distinctive way of life.

Sima has deep reservations about her daughter Maya's overreliance on her peers. This mother would like to see her daughter stand just a little more "on the edge": "What I miss a bit in her is some adventurousness, a little silliness, not to pay attention to the others but to say: 'So what, I won't be the best.' I think it's also an age thing—being worried about what her peers will say, what the world will say or what this imaginary other will say. In general, she is not very flexible. She has very rigid ethical codes of behavior."

Maya's "imaginary other" is for her entirely real, consisting of a coalition of her peer group, her school, her community, and her father (to whom Sima willingly defers with regard to her daughter's religious education). Sima too is grateful for having these "others" around, especially when they relieve her of some of the burden of her daughter's religious socialization: "It is comfortable for me to raise my children within a religious framework. What is permitted and prohibited become very simple and clear. There is a supreme power that helps you establish these boundaries. I use it rather cynically— in other words, intentionally—even though I also think there is intrinsic value in religion."

Like many other modern Orthodox parents, Sima "rather cynically" chose for her daughter a school more old-fashioned and single-minded than she herself would prefer. She knowingly abdicated her own voice in the religious education of her daughter.

These women's accounts of their roles in their daughters' religious educations all testify to a puzzling phenomenon. Instead of socializing their daughters themselves, many of them have chosen to rely on other people and institutions. This form of maternal abdication was not accidental, but consciously considered:

> "I chose to send her to Ulpana . . . because of my own weakness . . . because I was afraid . . . in spite of our adversarial relationship to the school."

> "I chose the school because its values are clear . . . even though I teach in Bet Sarah."

> "I chose not to gamble . . . She would be willing to conform. She would be willing to sacrifice herself."

> "My husband does the religious teaching in our home."

Even when the educational institution in question did represent the mother's religious convictions in some respect, often she would describe her choice of school as an act of abdication. The idea of *choosing* to abdicate indicates the complexity of the act involved. The questions that I asked do not have simple answers: How would women who abdicate respond to their own daughters' abdications? What would it mean for a mother not to abdicate? What would be the consequences for their daughters and for the tradition? What does it mean for a tradition to demand abdication for its continuity? Can a person sustain resistance together with commitment to the tradition, or does this combination invariably lead to abdication?

What message is being transmitted to daughters by their mothers' abdication?

"It Starts Resonating"

The most painful case of abdication among the Roman Catholic mothers I interviewed is of Ann, who with full consciousness decided to socialize her daughter within structured religion despite her experience of their parish as cruel and thus un-Christian. The story is worth telling in detail. Ann was, in her words, "in a very bad marriage." She sought and eventually was granted an annulment: "I wanted the annulment because, in our tradition, the sacrament [of marriage is an] opportunity to be blessed by God, and I felt the marriage was so destructive all the time that there was no blessing it. So it took the annulment to say it wasn't a sacrament."

During this time she was teaching in the Confraternity of Christian Doctrine (CCD) program in her church, as well as helping to run the confirmation program at the local parochial school. "I was happy because I was finally getting out of the marriage. I hadn't told my pastor, as it had nothing to do with him. The pastor called me in and said he didn't think he'd need my services because it would be so hard for me going through a divorce and still doing this other work. I was very angry. I was devastated. I went back and confronted him, and I did leave the parish."

Although Ann was told merely that her services as a teacher were no longer needed, she felt she could no longer belong to that parish. She noted that the response of the priest was different from the response of the principal of the school where she taught during the week. There the principal was completely supportive and told her she could stay and should stay, even though her husband "had complained to the powers that be, and they called my principal who had to call me in and say that this complaint had come that I was a divorced woman and I was teaching religion." Ann found a new parish that was "more inclusive—they have old people reading, and young people reading. They have women participating certainly as much as the Catholic Church allows. There's a gay man leading the choir."

And yet Ann sent her children back to CCD in her former parish on Sundays. She arranged custody so that the children would spend Sundays with their father "who is very Catholic—that is, he couldn't understand why I wanted out. This was like totally an enigma to him, that I could be so un-Catholic." Her husband, who had been very abusive for a long time, did not want to grant the divorce, as he believed in the "holiness of marriage." When it came to her children's religious education, however, Ann joined with her husband: "But we do think they should do their religious obligation. We agree on that. So I was relieved that he had that responsibility of taking them to church. It freed me." Ann, who knew that her church had shunned her—for leaving an abusive marriage, for feeling that it could not be considered a sacrament if there was abuse—still felt that her children needed to be part of that church, the community parish. She found a place for herself personally that was more inclusive, more spiritual and sensitive to religious needs, but when it came to her children's education, she stopped short. As Ann abdicates her socializing role as a religious mother, she feels that in some way she is doing what she must as a mother and hopes that someday she will be able to tell her daughter the story of her painful relationship with mainstream, establishment Catholicism.

The struggle to choose a religious education for their daughters was a complex process for the Catholic women, just as it was for the Jewish women. There was no simple solution available or, perhaps, even possible. How indeed would one begin to construct a school that would embody both the resisting self and the committed self that each mother wished for her daughters? The women have not avoided the pain or the ambivalence involved in the choice and have not averted their eyes from the price that their choices entail. These mothers are, in fact, hypervigilant concerning the possible consequences, immediate and remote, of their choices.

Seana chose a Catholic school for her daughters because "I wanted them to have some of what had nurtured me, and that was an experience of religious traditions. I wanted them to know 'Tantum Ergo,' and I wanted them to crown Mary. I wanted them to have those things that I felt had nurtured me, so I chose a Catholic school." Immediately after emphasizing the nurturing she remembered from her own experience, she almost recoiled in fear: "Oh my God, what have I done? I see a piece of rigidity. I see a holding-on doctrine. I see a narrowing of something. I say, 'Oh God, what am I doing?'" She described her situation as like an acrobat's: "I walk a tightrope . . . I see fundamental values, Catholic values that permeate everything—some of them I like and some of them I hate." She then goes beyond a generalized expression of satisfaction to a detailed list: "I like the value of the ritual. I like the smell. I like the words. I like the cave. I like those. I like crowning Mary. I listen to all of these Marion hymns. I listen to 'Handmaiden of the Lord.' I love *The Catholic Worker.* I love the notion of prayer . . . I want my girls to have all those things." Seana's senses are in play in describing her ambivalent relationship to her daughters' education. She feels comfortable with the music she hears, the aromas she smells, the warmth she feels; what she sees, however, alarms her. Whenever she "sees," she addresses God in startled guilt. In the interview, she continued this back-and-forth debate with herself, culminating in this summary:

> So I have all these things, and I want my girls to have all those things. I wanted them to have the value of faith, hope, and love, and I wanted them all their lives to struggle with what they mean. For me Catholicism had been this—you keep hitting against it. It's solid like a rock. Every time you hit against it, you have to say, "All right, where am I?

Am I knocked over? Am I still standing up? Where do I stand in reference to this thing that is so frigging immovable?" I have to give them the tradition for them to live with, for them to come up against.

Seana sees this view of education and this attitude toward her tradition as hers uniquely: "I find myself very separate from many other parents, who send their girls for answers," whereas she sends her girls "to struggle with" what their religion means. But interestingly, many of the other women I interviewed make the same claim.

The women were well aware that, if what they wanted was solely to educate their daughters to have an independent point of view and an autonomous voice, secular educational institutions were available. However, what these women hoped for was to enable their daughters to engage with a fuller range of live options, and the secular approach by definition excludes religion. They articulated the price of their choices.

Kathleen described an incident in which her daughter was made "to kneel down in the aisle" at school as "a penance" for some "mistake on her paper." "This is just so wrong," Kathleen said, "so utterly completely wrong." Her deepest concern was that her daughter "didn't tell me about it right away. I'm not sure," she added, "what her thinking was—other than maybe I would be upset with what she had done, that this was maybe the right punishment, whatever." Her fear was that her daughter had internalized the self that her teacher, "an elderly nun," had offered her: a bad girl who required humiliation as "penance."

Jacqueline, like many of the Jewish women, chose a more conservative school for her daughter than the one at which she taught. She "was concerned that [her daughter] would be turned off to the Catholic religion because [the teachers] were so conservative." It was an Opus Dei (an extremely conservative, even reactionary organization in the Catholic Church) school: "They had Mass every day, which is certainly not unusual. All the girls received the sacrament of penance, going to confession every week, and everybody did it. They would talk about what's the best way to tell a boy no." Many of the lay teachers "dedicated themselves to being celibate," and "some of the women . . . would wear those undershirts, those scratchy hair shirts." Jacqueline's daughter "thought that was terrible" but, like Kathleen's daughter, did not share her pain and confusion with her mother until she was older. Jacqueline spoke of this self-silencing with pain and confusion. Even so, Jacqueline continued to feel that the coalition she made between the more religious school, its teachers and her daughter was worthwhile because her daughter "did come away from there being very strong in her Catholic faith. And now she is more ready to hear other things, and question."

Once again, Jacqueline, like the other mothers, presents both sides vividly and lucidly, then concludes with an endorsement of her decision. On the one hand, she repeats her daughter's judgment: "They taught me the wrong things. They were too strict. They didn't let me know that some things were allowed." On the other hand, Jacqueline responds to her daughter's negative remarks with positive comments: "It was fine with me. I was very comfortable with what was being done there. I felt that there was really nothing wrong with being very conservative. I would rather that than being too liberal."

Catherine too is aware that, in the "fairly conservative" Catholic school where she sent her daughters, the girls would not be exposed to "the idea that people have different views." She was sarcastic about the school's traditional ethos: "You know, let's go over the benediction. Let's have the rosary . . . very much the 'yes father, oh father is right. Father rules the roost.'" In spite of this view, she believes that the school's "religious component [gave] them a faith that they can fall back on years later—we can say to them, 'There's a right and there's a wrong, and this is what we believe. And this has been our tradition.' That [capability], in the public schools, is much more limited."

Marianne had much the same thought. "I felt," she said, "that along with the struggle that we have in our home with children, raising children in this day, and that for them to hear some of the philosophies and thought and the beliefs that we espoused in our home, to have [those beliefs] with them every day, being taught to them in school, would also be another boost or another way that [those beliefs] would . . . [be] engrained in them."

In addition, the mothers tended to prefer Catholic schools because they are single-sex, holding that "it does a lot more for the self-esteem." Catherine continued: "And I really felt that in a small environment, an all-girls environment, she would have more of a chance to find who she is and to voice that . . . They can take on leadership roles. It's okay for them to achieve in science and math. [In] the public school here," Catherine added, "you have to deal with that boy/girl part: How do I look? Is he attracted to me now? Is he attractive to me?" Marianne also expressed the view that an all-girls school enabled her daughter to have "more of a focus on her self, on her strengths and what she can . . . become, without some of the other distractions."

Some of the Catholic mothers resonated with what the Jewish mothers had told me about school choice. Catherine in particular articulated an affinity with that position. "It starts resonating," she said. "Yes, very much . . . I wouldn't say I'm ultratraditional. I wouldn't say I'm ultramodern either . . . And that is a plus side, that they're going to a traditional grammar school, that they can see both sides."

Many mothers, Catholic and Jewish both, found that the only choice that would lead to continuity was an education that broke with aspects of their own complex views, understanding of nuances, and, above all, feelings of disenfranchisement and alienation as women. They feared what one Catholic woman termed "rocklike rigidity" and what a Jewish woman called "the hard-headed Israeli approach," but they appeared to have concluded that they and their daughters must pay the price of conformity first, because the young require a firm base. Metaphors of hardness and solidity were repeatedly used. They must also pay because the mothers need obedient girls as well, since it frees them to explore their own complex attitudes toward tradition.

Good Enough Mothering: A Path to Resistance

The mothers, both Catholic and Jewish, all experienced a delayed but deep irritation about their role as women. Miriam claimed that had I interviewed the women in their late teens, I would have met with a very different group. She pointed out that most of the women experienced significant change in their thirties rather than in their teens. She attributed this delayed resistance, in the case of the Jewish women, to the influence of Israeli youth movements and the general cultural ethos of conformity to ideologies. (Most young Israelis join ideological youth movements that have clear prescriptive social ideals and codes of behavior.) Miriam claims that these women were conformists before marriage, but one could argue that they are even now adult versions of "good girls." They live not on the fringe but within the boundaries of traditional religious communities. They teach in established religious institutions. They dress modestly, and most of the Jewish women cover their hair in compliance with tradition. They all do their best to ensure that their daughters become, like themselves, good girls.

The Catholic women conform to their community's standards for good women and mothers, as well. They attend Mass regularly, are active in their parishes as Eucharistic ministers and teachers, send their daughters to parochial schools, and clearly take their religious lives seriously. But this is not how these mothers see themselves. They see themselves as having experienced radical changes in their beliefs and identities vis-à-vis their pasts, their traditions, and their tradition's myths, sacred texts, and attitudes toward women *after* they were married and had children.[2] Perhaps they felt free and secure enough to question their respective traditions only after (and conceivably because) they had fulfilled what they believed their communities expected of them. Even in their questioning, these women as teachers continue to socialize adolescent girls other than their own daughters within the very culture that they question.

Abdication is not necessarily a sign of powerlessness. As I see it, these mothers' choice of abdication with respect to their daughters' educations reflects their power (and their perception of their power) to determine their daughters' future relationship to the tradition. Being married, having children, and living within the recognized religious frameworks of their communities allow them to raise questions. They have all, as it were, paid their dues. They cannot be browbeaten into believing their questions will lead to the breakdown of traditional values, because their daily lives embody these values. Marriage and other institutions have enabled them to be resisters, to listen to other voices challenging the status quo. There is a conservative safety net that enables them to experiment.

One might speculate that if their daughters were also resisters, they, as mothers, would not have felt sufficiently secure to take risks. Good daughters certify good mothers. Raising good girls is both a way of protecting daughters and an insurance policy for mothers. While these women express disappointment in their daughters' conformity, they are more than a little relieved by its consequences: they want to transmit their tradition along with a sense of distance. They want their daughters to fulfill what orthodoxy demands, but ambivalently. The message is, "Do what is expected of you. Continue this tradition, but don't feel too good about it." Their challenge is how to raise active and full-fledged yet critical members of the community. As they themselves have done, they want their daughters to master the fine art of standing at a distance—but by no means beyond the boundaries of community. By *almost* abdicating their role as the major socializers of their daughters—by accepting the role of good enough mother—these women may have paved the way for their daughters to begin to question, though perhaps not until they reach their mothers' ages. Thus continuity makes ambiguity possible.

The Ideal Good Girl

What are the similarities and differences between the women's expectations of their daughters and the communities' definitions of "good girl"? Asking the mothers to define the ideal good girl was a way of learning about their perceptions of their community's values in relation to their own. Is there a difference between how they judge themselves and their daughters with respect to the community's ideal of the good girl? Are they as critical about their daughter's socialization as they are about their own?

Bruria is the most articulate about the disparity between her own and the community's ideals. Her culture's expectations of girls, she says, is that they become nonpeople. "They expect nothing from girls," she complains. "It is enough that she does *not* do things. She should not desecrate the Sabbath. She should not be wild." Girls should be known by what they are not, by the noise they do not make. In other words, she says, girls are not to be known at all. Bruria herself abhors the passive model of the woman whose religiosity is contingent on men's religious life. She expects her own daughters to observe all the *mitzvot* (commandments), even those from which women have traditionally been exempt. Her interpretation of the principle that women are exempt from time-dependent *mitzvot* is simply that women are free to not do these things but that they should do them if they can make the time.

When asked for a positive definition of the good girl, one that goes beyond critique, Bruria became almost surprisingly abstract. She must, Bruria said, "be a good person, an honest person, deeply connected to her tradition. The values she lives by should have practical implications. Her actions should reflect these values."

Some of the Catholic women were equally abstract and vague. Kathleen began with an ethereal definition: "I think, for me, I think a good girl is someone who takes her own life seriously. And by that I mean someone who has an interior life . . . For me in the Catholic community, it's one who has a relationship with her God, but she experiences [it] in community. Which is the ritual community. But also beyond that, [it] should bring her outside to interact with the world. And to try to repair that world."

Pressed to provide the definition of good girl prevailing in her community, Kathleen offered credible details about her generation rather than her daughter's: "I think things changed very much . . . A good girl didn't gossip. A good girl didn't say unkind things about people. A good girl made sure she went to church every Sunday, and a good girl was very careful of her language. A good girl was not affectionate in public with her boyfriend. She would also not have a steady boyfriend. She would smile a lot—whatever it was that she was told."

Kathleen was obviously uncomfortable with the notion of obedience as an integral part of her tradition. She said, "One doesn't want written on her tombstone, 'She was a good girl and did everything she was told,'" but in fact obedience was a common theme among the Catholic women when asked to define a good girl in Catholic terms:

> "A good girl obeys. There's a lot of obedience. I would not want my daughter to be obedient." (Sandra)

> "Be someone submissive. Defer to authority. Those are all the good girl things. But I don't want them to be submissive. I want them to question authority." (Catherine)

"Obedience—to everyone in authority. My girls are still going
to struggle with the good girl [model], but I don't think the
Catholic Church is the only place imposing that on them."
(Seana)

Obedience for the Catholic women seems to be a character trait, a
characteristic of submissiveness. It is for them a negative trait, one
that they do not want their daughters to exemplify, but a trait
nonetheless required by their tradition.

The Jewish women tended to respond to my promptings by defining the good girl in very precise terms, implying that goodness is
more a matter of behavior than a defining trait of character: "A good
girl in Beit Ariel [her community] wears long skirts, never miniskirts,
a little bit of makeup, a stylish haircut but not freaky, not colored or
punk. She never combs her hair with lots of gel or looks punk,
because that is not accepted. It would never even cross her mind."

Although the girls in Sima's community may read magazines and
newspapers and watch television, they have a picture of how they
ought to appear that is so clear it would never cross their minds to
look otherwise. A good girl not only refrains from sexual behavior,
but also looks virginal. While she need not appear sexless like some
of the ultra-Orthodox, she does not wear jeans or pants. She wears
denim skirts hemmed at knee-level or lower. She may have her hair
styled fashionably—she does not wear long braids as is the practice
in ultra-Orthodox circles—but fashionably, within definite limits.
The good girl is patriotic and serves in the army or in Sherut Le'umi,
the alternative national service framework for religious girls. "An
intelligent and good girl reads books and listens to classical music,"
Sima adds, "but even if she herself doesn't listen to classical music,
she knows that it is considered better music than Israeli or American
rock."

Sima feels relatively comfortable with the accepted definition of a
good girl. She would not mind her daughter's wearing pants, but she

knows that "it would never even cross her mind"; she dresses like the other girls in her milieu. "For me," Sima says, "a good girl is polite. The teachers tell me that all my children are well behaved, so I guess I do transmit that message pretty strongly."

Rachel's description of the good girl was also basically congruent with her community's values. The qualifications she added suggested that, while her own views might deviate somewhat from the accepted norms, she was not willing to make an issue of these differences. When discussing the norm of girls getting married in their early twenties, her ambivalence was apparent: "To say that it is an ideal of mine that she be married by twenty-five is difficult. If she won't, I would be sorry but . . . An ideal is something that—theoretically— you say is correct and desired. I am not sure I would say that . . . But practically speaking, my answer would be yes."

While "practically" saying "yes" to the community's norm of early marriage, Rachel felt the need to indicate where she differed: "A good girl should be independent, not dependent on what others think of her." For Rachel herself this independence was expressed as ambivalence. She accepted the socially sanctioned age for marriage, but not as a matter of personal conviction, and this was consistent with her ambivalent feelings about her daughters' education. She wanted them to finish most of their education before marriage, but she realized that putting off marriage to a later age might make finding a good match more difficult.

Elisheva's way of expressing her ambivalence was to claim that she was not, like many of the mothers, officially part of any particular community. "I used to live on a kibbutz, where there were clear definitions." Compared to her kibbutz, the city presented her with no identifiable community standard. Nonetheless, she was prepared to offer her own definition of the good girl: "For me the most important thing is personal integrity and honesty—not to live in a reality of double standards, not to think one thing and say another. The dress codes are a bit funny. They are not allowed to wear pants in school, but afterwards most of the girls do wear pants. I find this absurd. I do not wear pants, but I think it is fine for my daughter to wear pants. Pants are modest. I don't like short skirts."

While emphasizing personal integrity and honesty, and rejecting the hypocrisy of many of her religious friends with respect to modest dress and *lashon hara* (gossip), Elisheva appeared to know what the community standards were and accepted her daughter's conformity to them. "I think she is a very good girl," Elisheva said positively, but then quickly added: "Sometimes she has to pay a price for being so good. I think she silences herself to fit our standards of goodness." Although as a mother Elisheva was aware of the painful experience of female socialization, the importance of producing a good girl was predominant: "I think she silences herself to fit our standards of goodness"—an alliance between "I" and "they" have molded "her" according to "our" standards of goodness.

The Jewish mothers tended to respond to my question about the ideal good girl in terms of dress and grooming or public comportment, while the Catholic women also spoke of sexual norms. "That was very much evident," Kathleen said about the norms of good girlhood maintained in Catholic schools, "that a good girl was not sexually active." Yehudit made somewhat similar remarks about the Jewish community: "Meeting boys, sexual attractions, choosing a husband . . . I would be happy if she were to go out more. I haven't discouraged her going out. I think it is something that needs practice. But, a good girl basically has her mind on other things."

"The [good girl] model is not an oppressive model," Yehudit said regarding the cultural ideal of no premarital sex—with one minor exception: "The one aspect which I think is problematic is the lack of sufficient opportunities for boys and girls to mix—which is based on the assumption that it will happen at the right time, whatever the circumstances."

Havva and Shoshi felt no hesitation in describing their daughters as good girls. "She is a good student," Havva said of Tami. "She has the right sort of ideals, and she is not wild." The only hint of criticism in her description of Tami was her suggestion that her daughter might have internalized the social ideal too completely: "I think it would be terrible if she left the kitchen too neat. Then she would be *too* good. It was good to see her becoming a little impertinent. She was thrown out of class. I was happy about that . . . Of course, she stood by the door taking notes."

Shoshi's response was the most unequivocal: "My daughter is the embodiment of the good girl both by the community's standards and by my own. She does extremely well in school. She is very accepted in her class. For me, caring for others is the important criterion for being a good girl."

Indeed most of the Jewish and Catholic women, despite individual differences, expressed satisfaction with their daughters' socialization in accordance with the prevailing community ideal. The women's narratives about the ideal good girl referred repeatedly to the primary distinction I heard throughout these interviews: the community ideal versus their own. For some women these were identical; others emphasized their preference for their own ideals. It appeared at first that each woman had defined "good girl" differently because each spoke from her particular perspective. Most, however, seemed to agree with the definitions of the others.

Each was explicit about those aspects of the community ideal with which she disagreed, but the general thrust for each was that she did not see the community's standards and her own as conflicting or even discontinuous. While teachers by profession, these women do not perceive themselves either as defining the rules on their own or as enforcing a heteronomous "father's rule" (i.e., external dictates of the patriarchy). Raising children in accordance with their communities' ideal, on the whole, is not experienced as a form of capitulation.

Their aspirations for their daughters' futures are, for the most part, traditional. "I hope she marries someone like my husband," Yehudit said, "someone who is sensitive, caring, and who shares the workload at home." They want their daughters to have families and children, and all expressed the hope that their daughters would remain religious, although some defined this rather vaguely. Elisheva spoke of her daughter's life having a "religious dimension." While all said they would not disown their daughters if they were to become nonreligious, that certainly would be very painful for these mothers and would evoke feelings of personal failure.

All the mothers wanted their daughters to be "self-fulfilled." Their definitions were clearly culture-bound or, rather, bound to culture. As they see it, the self is not an atomic entity, and thus self-fulfillment must take place within community, family, nation, synagogue, or church. Several women explicated their ideals in the terms of a feminist ethos.[3] Rachel corrected herself when she heard herself use the term "self-fulfillment," immediately distinguishing between the Western ideal of the individual self as an end in itself and the notion of the self as fulfilled only within the context of relationships and commitments. Bruria described self-fulfillment in terms of her feminist understanding of Judaism. She said that she could not imagine her daughter fulfilled without a religious life as active as that of men, even if this meant making some men in her world uncomfortable. Elisheva stressed that her daughter should choose a fulfilling career, independent of what a "good husband" might appreciate, even if this meant delaying marriage for a few years. All of the women, Jewish and Catholic, qualified the hope that their daughters marry by stressing that they do not want their daughters to sacrifice their own careers for the sake of marriage. They also believe that men are changing and that not all men subscribe to the old stereotypes of "appropriate" women's careers.

Notably, none of the women expressed a hope that her daughter become rich. For them, money is more an instrument than an end in itself, and they tend, as teachers, to have modest incomes. They did, however, express the hope that their daughters' lives as women would be easier than their own. They hoped that their daughters would be able to balance motherhood and a career more easily than they had done. Elisheva still painfully felt that there was no reason to believe that her daughter would not "fall into the same catch that I fell into. After all," in spite of her hopes she concluded with resignation, "it is the destiny of all women. We have no way out."

Life versus Law

Traditional religions such as Orthodox Judaism and Roman Catholicism assert authority over all areas of life, so, on the face of it, there would seem to be no room for individual difference, initiative, or change. The women in this study all regard themselves as Orthodox Jews or faithful Catholics. Their answer to my questions about what governs their lives and sets the criteria for their behavior was quite clear from the outset. "I live according to Halakhah," or "I live according to Church teachings," were their immediate, unqualified responses. Yet, despite what sounds like a categorical commitment, the discussions soon revealed many areas where they struggled to find a path of their own. Even in situations where the Halakhah or canon law was unambiguous, they seemed to be searching for different rules, ones that would accord better with their individual convictions and with their daughters' changing needs.

The women were aware that this uncertainty could be interpreted as inconsistency or a lack of faith by those who expect coherence and obedience; but the commitment to religion and the commitment to an inner voice coexist at a very deep level of their identities. While they live in communities that accept religious norms according to the rabbinic tradition or to the Church, they also feel claimed by a world of human needs and values that sometimes conflict with formal religious constraints. On the whole, however, the women believe that such conflicts can be resolved within the system. This conviction is among one of their defining characteristics. For these groups of women, secular experience is a significant aspect of their life, their way of thinking and feeling.

Not every element foreign to a tradition can be integrated into it even by the most creative of interpretations, and this hard reality led these women and others like them into formidable difficulties and serious dilemmas. They feel compelled to choose between different parts of their selves or, in Yehudit's words, between life (individual selfhood) and law (orthodoxy). This formulation may seem weighted in favor of a particular solution ("I find myself favoring the life side of the life-versus-law antithesis," Yehudit says), but any decision is accompanied and followed by feelings of ambiguity and uncertainty.

All of the women knew that there are no simple solutions to problems resulting from their complex cultural identities and that religious tradition is as much a dimension of the problems as of the solutions. Furthermore, for them, the "synthesis" between modernity and tradition offered by modern-Orthodox Judaism or of the post–Vatican II Church was less than perfect. Tensions remained, sometimes forcing a choice between orthodoxy and modernity, law and life. They often expressed the conviction that their religious needs as women could be fulfilled if the spirit of the religious system were realized with greater sensitivity. They blamed the rabbinate, the Church hierarchy, and even their own communities for active and passive resistance to change. Paradoxically, the women expressed deep antipathy toward the institutions of religious authority, while expecting the rabbis and priests themselves to initiate change. These women feel frustration toward those who can—but refuse to—reinterpret canonical texts and legislation in a way that could help make their identities whole. These women are well aware of the mechanisms for legitimate change and that an elite group of men control these mechanisms, and so feel disempowered to bring it about.

Several of the Catholic women, for example, explicitly remarked on the reticence of the clergy to initiate life-affirming change and compared contemporary priests' attitudes unfavorably with what they viewed as the all-embracing, nonjudgmental, undogmatic love of Jesus for his followers. Seana questioned "all the ways in which the Church has turned itself" away from New Testament values and said that often the Church "must make Jesus roll over in his grave. Jesus would say, 'What are you talking about? I talked about love'—the Church just doesn't get it." While the Church does not "get it," Seana feels she does. She was clearly concerned about the hierarchy's claim to expert authority. "I have a masters in religious education, and I taught in Catholic school," she says—but she refused to unlearn what life, her own experiences, taught her. Other women associate their secular educations with life and the Church with law. Some accept the findings of modern behavioral science as equal to, or even truer than, the doctrine of their religion. Kathleen asserted: "I read a lot . . . and I just believe that there is a methodology in psychology that hasn't been totally accepted yet . . . There are suppositions that are held in the Church—well they're more than suppositions—there are laws promulgated. I just think that there is a certain official stance that hasn't allowed other educated experiences to be held as true."

Even where the problem seems a matter of conflicting educations, and thus intellectual, the clash of life and law is intensely personal and is often reformulated as an opposition between *my life* and an external normative tradition. Notwithstanding the women's deep identification with Halakhah or Church teaching, problematic situations are experienced as personal confrontations between *my* autonomous voice—*my* understanding of what serves *my* or *my daughter's* happiness—and *their* voice—the impersonal, heteronomous voice of the clergy. The ambiguities these women face may thus extend beyond specific issues in question to the very basis of their relationship with tradition.

One of the topics that invariably elicited this kind of crisis reaction among the women I interviewed was the subject of their daughters' sexuality. Elisheva vacillated between not-knowing and knowing, between self-doubt and confidence, between what "we do" and what "I think." Her existential dilemma seemed to take the form of an internal debate between the two parties—the two voices—in the discussion:

> Look, we live according to Halakhah, and therefore I don't think it is a good idea to have premarital sex. However, on some level I think there is a correlation between age and sex. If my daughter comes to me at 29 and is still unmarried, it is different. I don't know, but it is different.

First Voice.   Elisheva accepts Halakhic restrictions on sexual activity before marriage. She presents the law as a premise, but then qualifies her conclusion in a subjective mode:

- "Look": the normative force of Halakhah is visible, objective, public, clear-cut.

- "We live according to Halakhah": We = I + she + they, an assemblage of subjectivities; Halakhah = the objective public system.

- "And therefore I don't think it is a good idea": a rather weak, subjective statement of Elisheva's submission to objective authority.

Second Voice.   There are situations where non-Halakhic considerations would be legitimate:

- "However": despite the strength of the first position taken, there are alternatives.

- "On some level": the alternatives are not as "visible" and public as Halakhah; they exist "on some level" (below the surface?).

- "I think there is a correlation": a more positive and definite statement than "I don't think it is a good idea . . ." The opaque, non-Halakhic alternatives produce a more positive conclusion than the clear, objective Halakhah.

Elisheva is aware that her daughter's needs might lead one day to their both accepting a set of rules not based on religious law. Since Halakhah does not recognize this situation as a valid exception to its rules prohibiting premarital sex, Elisheva should draw the conclusion that her two premises are incompatible. But, while she realizes the implication logically of juxtaposing these premises, she is less than certain about the conclusion she herself may reach:

- "I don't know": a cautious expression of uncertainty.

- "But": a change of direction, a transition.

- "It is different": a definite expression of certainty.

Elisheva's predicament involves not only her own conflict with what "we" (I + they) do but also her daughter's (we = I + she). She believes that her daughter knows about her ambivalence. While her daughter knows that her mother endorses the Halakhic position on premarital sex, she also knows that Elisheva believes there are situations where other, non-Halakhic considerations might take precedence over current Halakhic practice.

Elizabeth likewise senses a distinction between the personal moral voice, her voice or anyone's, and that of her religion, Roman Catholicism. "I grew up listening to a lot of that rhetoric," she says of the absolutist language of Church teachings on sex:

I think if we're all to follow a path of truth for ourselves, to find our own truth . . . and it's difficult for me to say what somebody else's path is and why they should take that path and why they should not take this path, so sometimes I'm not very happy with where the Church crosses that line into moral issues . . . I know that, traditionally, religion has a place in all the moral issues of the times, and I see that as valuable, but I see it as too rigid, on the other hand, and I would like to see some balance there. I think maybe . . . the people will bring that need to religion, and I think that when we're all better versed and better in touch with it and know for ourselves what the real truth is, . . . religion will move to a higher place.

Elizabeth speaks of three truths here, in an almost Hegelian pattern: There is "our own truth [hers and 'somebody else's']," the Church's truth, and then eventually the "real truth," which, when it emerges, will transcend the prior antithetical truths.

Bruria also speaks of a future when authorities (in her case, rabbanic) will hear the claims that women are making on them and will change existing law. She too holds out the possibility of a synthesis, when Halakhah will at last move forward. But today, as she mothers her daughter, she is faced with a stark either/or alternative. Bruria is not bothered by the differences between Halakhic and modern attitudes toward sex independent of marriage, as long as the issue involves only her own life. She does not feel the need to rationalize her living according to Halakhic norms and feels comfortable explaining her way of life as a personal choice between legitimate alternatives. The difficulty arises for her, however, when she comes to realize that her daughter may not choose as she did:

We are speaking of two conflicting frameworks. The Halakhic framework looks positively on relationships between men and women but only within the confines of marriage . . . Sexuality is beautiful but only within the marital framework . . . The Western point of view tells us that meaningful, loving relationships between men and women are possible outside of marriage. These are two standpoints—each has its own logic, its own truth . . . but one has to make a choice.

Bruria's choice is to adopt the Halakhic standpoint without denouncing other values systems. I read this passage from my interviews with Bruria to one of the Catholic interviewees, Catherine, and she was less persuaded than Bruria that the modern point of view on sex is valid. "Those same 'meaningful relationships,'" Catherine said, "are the ones that end. There is no commitment. But I think the majority of people really do believe in the whole messing around. I think that's where faith and religion, those traditions, become very countercultural. And that we need to say to the kids: 'That is not the way; this is the way.'"

The difference between Catherine and Bruria regarding the possibility of premarital sex narrows when Bruria considers the choices her own daughter will one day make. "As a person," Bruria says, "I completely understand and endorse the Halakhic perspective. But," she continues, "what would I do if my daughter did not?" The connecting "but" raises the issue of whether Bruria "as a person" was the same as Bruria as a mother: "Since it has not arisen as a real issue, it is easy for me to be generous and say I would accept her no matter what. I would like to state my opinion and, even if it were not accepted, maintain a close relationship with her. If she does not accept the path that I have chosen, I hope that we will accept each other, that she will not see me as narrow-minded, and I will not see her as cheap."

While Bruria was hoping for continuity, and spending enormous energies on educating and convincing her daughter about the beauty of an Halakhic way of life, she was aware that her daughter might eventually choose differently and did not believe that their relationship should be contingent on religious continuity. She also felt that issues of sexuality should not be made into a test case of a person's overall commitment to Judaism: "It is important for me to stress that I am not that uptight about her virginity. That's not the issue . . . Virginity is a very formal thing. What I care about is her whole acceptance of the framework."

Bruria was not completely sure that she could overcome her feelings of loss and betrayal if her daughter had sexual relationships outside marriage, but she hoped that she would be able to accept her daughter's choice. Although mothering cannot be separated from religious culture, this is precisely what many of the women hoped. To be in society, women must in some sense abdicate their selves; to be fully themselves, they must change their society. This is an untoward crisis faced by mothers who begin to socialize their children and realize the improbability of their task while remaining true to themselves.

Perhaps another way of making this point is to argue, as Havva did in our interview, that religious law falls short of prescribing the ideal form of human relationship. Although qualifying her views on sexuality with a prudent "it's an individual thing," Havva was quite confident that modern psychological opinion is reliable:

> I think that it's not good to grow up without loving and without experiencing close feelings for someone else, whether or not they are sexual . . . Sexuality in the fullest sense is important in order to have a good marriage, in order to pick a partner, in order to understand a person. (I'm not talking about what you see on TV where people jump into bed, look at each other, and if they like the face, . . . check out the rest of the body the same evening.) It should not be done lightly. But in a serious relationship, you can't cut off this part (although I understand and I respect people who can learn about each other without it). It is a conflict, though. And there's nothing you can do about it. You have to live with that conflict, or you have to make a decision one way or another.

Although Havva felt that Halakhah does not answer life's needs in terms of the deepest relationships between men and women, she was not derisive of the Halakhic viewpoint as she was of the television attitude toward sexuality. Still, she clearly held that Halakhah can be detrimental to human relationships. She mentioned the possible negative consequences of a couple's first getting "to know each other" (in the biblical sense) after marriage. As for herself, Havva did not observe all the laws of sexual abstinence within marriage (specifically, during menstruation), though she still went to the *mikveh* (ritual bath) (see Biale 1984, Ellinson 1992, and Greenberg 1990). She acknowledged that she made compromises in this area of Halakhic observance and that, rather than attempt to resolve the conflict, she had somehow learned to live with it.

The conflict of life-versus-law is sharpest when the claims made in the name of life are said to be based in objective science. The controversy over homosexuality and the family is a case in point. "On the one hand," as Bruria put it, "psychology tells us that homosexuality is an innate trait, so how can one call something that someone has no control over 'an abomination,' as the Bible does? On the other hand, the Halakhah is very clear that the family must be made up of a male and female parent and must replicate itself. A way has to be found for the Halakhah to retain its values of the normative family and the continuation of society while at the same time allowing for individual differences."

"A way has to be found" to resolve this quandary because, with the pressures of modern society, the issue of homosexuality can no longer be discussed within the framework of the Bible alone. For Bruria, calling an act an "abomination" implies that it is done freely and without coercion, external or internal. She attributes scientific authority to modern psychology and takes for granted that its findings about the innate factors underlying homosexuality must be absorbed before making a judgment. Bruria thus operated within two seemingly incompatible frameworks. As she saw matters, scientific knowledge does not necessarily undermine the normative

Halakhic family but does call its exclusivity into question. Bruria said she hoped that it would become possible to live according to both life and law, but when I asked her whom she would expect to initiate the necessary legal changes, she could not give me a clear answer. Since changes in Halakhah must be made by legal authorities, she did not feel personally empowered, but she believed that the rabbis would not act unless there was pressure from the community at large.

Homosexuality was for many of the Catholic women an issue that made them feel at odds with the Church—or in some cases, confused. Marianne said of her own confusion that "maybe I should be more staunch on that or 'make up your mind,' but I just don't feel with certain things I can do that." She did not believe that sexual preference defines one's being: "That's not their soul and their spirit and who they are. It's just [that] I have a hard time with that . . . I can't say I consider that sinful, or something that would be bad, or [something] that the Church should look at as bad." She immediately personalized the question: "Because if it was one of my children, I would feel terrible if people called them bad just because of that."

For Marianne the issue is complex; it becomes still more confusing when she sees it through her mothering lens. However, there is a voice calling her out of her confusion. In her narrative, when that voice enters, Marianne loses her "self" or I-voice and moves suddenly into a "you" or a second-person voice. This second-person voice is ushered in by a "should." When the "should" arrives, a commandment follows. The voice of command instructs her: "make up your mind." This voice has a clear stance and demands equal clarity from her. Although she was taught a simple truth, a human component makes it impossible for her to see the issue unidimensionally. Yet, one could interpret her confusion itself as a stance, a complex human stance as opposed to a single "bad-good" judgment. It is possible, indeed, that Marianne *has* made up her mind. She has decided that the issue is more complex than the Church asserts: "But I just don't feel with certain things I can do that." She cannot apply terms like "sinful" or "bad" to these intensely personal issues.

Catherine, on the other hand, was clearer about her positions. She spoke to me of a woman and a priest that were dealing with gays: "They had been sanctioned for not supporting the Church's view enough. They were told they no longer could work with this program of ministering to gays. They also could not hold any office within their own orders . . . Their teaching supported the Catholic Church's view, but it didn't shake the finger at gays, saying, 'mean, awful, horrible, sinful person.'"

I described, for Catherine, Bruria's sense of divided loyalty on the question of homosexuality, her feeling of division between the truth as defined by modern psychology and the truth as defined in Leviticus. In response, Catherine invoked Jesus as her support against the Bible's condemnation of homosexual acts: "Christ's teachings often went to this: What is more important, following the letter of the law or following the spirit of the law? . . . [He was] addressing the person, and the person needing to feel whole and worthy. Isn't that more important than shaking your finger at them and saying No! Gotta go with the spirit of the law more than the strict law . . . I've had friends who are gay, and I do feel very strongly . . . They're people first."

As we have seen, religious mothers are often hesitant about exposing their children to their most liberal opinions, but Catherine was insistent: "My kids are very strongly brought up in their faith that it's not okay to make fun of people who are gay." Catherine had no qualms about accepting scientific over religious authority on this question: "A whole lot of the attitude and the problems would disappear if we could say, 'You know what, it's okay' . . . exactly as this woman [Bruria] said. If psychologically we're saying, 'Oh yeah, it makes perfect sense,' then *we* are where the problem is coming from.

[Homosexuality, itself, is] not the issue. It's been around for years and years."

Marianne shares Catherine's attitude toward homosexuality but, unlike Catherine, is apprehensive about the possible consequences. "There are very few things," she states, "that I can look at and say: 'Now that is really bad. Do not ever do that.'" But she wonders if this belief in moral ambiguity may lead her to feel that all behavior is legitimate. "I get a little scared with ambiguity," she says. "I worry . . . that if I don't say this is right or this is wrong" to her children, they will go astray. "But at the same time I don't feel comfortable making those statements."

Marianne's ambivalence was more typical of the Catholic women I spoke with than Catherine's liberal certainty. More commonly, these women expressed certainty followed by fear; they find the rigidity of religious doctrine or law discomforting, but find the results of flexibility perhaps even less acceptable. As Marianne remarked: "What I used to think was 'absolutely definitely, definitely, definitely.' Now I feel like I'm sometimes standing on sand, as opposed to on really hard ground." A position of definite opposition to a Church doctrine—to the doctrine of a Church that Jesus built "upon a rock"—often leads to a feeling of instability or disintegration.

For the Catholic women I interviewed, unlike for the Jewish women, the point of greatest disagreement with their clergy, and the point of greatest instability therefore, was the regulation of sexual behavior. For the Catholic women, this was the crossroads of life and law. They in general felt the Church's regulation of sex was obsessive, sometimes bizarre, and usually intolerable. Marianne indeed dismissed the subject as a "Catholic School hang-up," and Seana condescended to what she called "the guilties" as an overriding feature of Catholic education. Lucy said that even women sworn to celibacy found "the preoccupation in our tradition with sexual matters" off-putting: "I teach scripture to young nuns," she told me, "and one of them came to me and said, 'If the only thing we talk about is the mystery of sex, isn't there more to this? Who would be drawn to a tradition that is so preoccupied?'" But sexual "preoccupation" was not the only problem; the women found the doctrinal and legal content of the preoccupation problematic.

Discussion of sexuality among the Catholic women centered on the issues of birth control[4] and abortion.[5] Neither topic ever came up in discussion with the Jewish women. Jewish law is quite flexible when it comes to birth control, especially for women living in the modern Orthodox context. Although it is a *mitzvah,* a commandment, to have children, planning pregnancy is not a sin. The onus of birth control is on the woman in that the use of condoms is not allowed. It is not permissible for a man to destroy his own sperm. Passive means of preventing conception, for example, by a woman using birth control such as the pill or an IUD, do not constitute a Halakhic problem. The open question is whether a delay in fulfilling the commandment of bringing children into the world is permissible.

There is more than one opinion on this question within the rabbinate (disagreement among authorities is a feature of Jewish law, unlike in Roman Catholic jurisprudence), and there are many Orthodox rabbis who will indeed allow women to use birth control in cases of physical and even psychological stress. Whether a human life begins at conception is, moreover, not so clear in Jewish law; thus, while abortion is not treated lightly by the rabbis, there is no equation of abortion and murder. There are times when rabbis permit abortions. The status of an infant under one month of age is also unclear: Jewish law does not require the rituals of mourning for an infant who dies within thirty days after birth. Furthermore, in Israel, an abortion is legal and accessible to almost all who request one. Abortion has not been an issue of public debate or controversy, then, under either the religious or the civil law.

But for the Catholic women, who live in the context of Pope Paul VI's encyclical *Humanae Vitae,* with its prohibition of all unnatural forms of birth control and of abortion under any circumstances, these were questions that aroused strong feelings. Considerable bitterness was expressed about the fact that men without children had control over reproduction and a "right" to pass judgment. Sandra felt she spoke for many: "That is really how many Catholics feel on birth control. We feel when the pope has raised toddlers, we will listen. My mother's favorite joke is, Mrs. Murphy, who has eleven children, is screaming at her children, and the local priest just comes by, and she has lost it, and the priest says, 'Mrs. Murphy, remember the Holy Family,' and she says, 'Yeah, her and her *one!*'"

The same sentiment was expressed with the same passion by Seana, who said, as though addressing the hierarchy: "Don't talk to me about birth control. Give me a break! What do you know? You're sitting up with your little hat on . . . You don't have a clue. Every priest should be required to live one month in a family, and someone in the family has to have one of those really bad throw-up viruses."

There was agreement among the women I interviewed that the alienation of women from the clergy on the matter of birth control was almost total. Sandra promised that "if there is an American Catholic who doesn't practice birth control, I'll give . . . a million dollars to the person who can find her." She felt in fact that use of birth control was so widespread that the legal authority of the Church was now widely perceived as illegitimate.

Marianne raised the matter of birth control in explicitly, though diffidently, feminist terms: "I don't know whether that's about womanhood . . . and our free will now, and that we don't have to listen to a man to say, 'This is right or wrong, this is what you have to do or what you don't have to do' . . . If nothing else, that is one of the things that feminism brought around, even within the Catholic Church. To say, 'nobody can tell me that I should have fifteen children.' You know what I mean? I don't know, I don't even think that God would want me to have fifteen or twenty children . . . I don't know, I don't know."

Marianne's repeated claim not to know for certain where she stood with respect to birth control was belied by her radical summary: "But I don't feel any allegiance or obedience to that [Humanae Vitae]." She invoked God on the side of women against the all-male clergy. In the life versus law formula, life and God were for Marianne on one side, law and men on the other. The situation was quite different for Kathleen who claimed that the Church itself in fact endorsed birth control—or at least accepted it as a possibility. In her view, then, the Church was on the side of life as opposed to law:

> The Church teaches many things—so that there's a wide variety of teachings on this issue. The Church does not condemn birth control. Actually the Church has developed a program called Natural Family Planning, which is . . . we're talking about, birth control. It's cast in a different light, and more and more people are talking about women being in touch with their own bodies, understanding their own cycle, but then again the burden is on the woman. They talk very sincerely about the relationship between husband and wife in this and participating in this program together. I think the people involved are very sincere about it. I think it's one way.

Most of the women, however, did not feel that the Church gave them a real birth control option with Natural Family Planning because it is not reliable. When Catherine was younger, she struggled because, although she knew she was not ready to have children, she was a product of a "Catholic school training of never crossing what the Church had said." She recalled the struggle as like being pulled between a rational self that told her that she needed to wait to be a mother and a feeling of duty and allegiance to what she had been taught:

I mean, I knew in my head what I was doing was right. I knew that unprepared women make inadequate mothers. [However,] in my heart it was a struggle between teachings. But I was not quite ready. Now I can look at that and say I made the right decision to delay motherhood . . . And I think that I've matured to say: "You know what? The Church is an institution, and even an institution can make mistakes on issues. My struggle with the Catholic Church has been [that] they've made good decisions, but they haven't always been, like, on the ball of where they should be. Sometimes they feel rather oppressive . . . their traditions and their views and what they've done. I can look now and say: "Wow, the Church did make a few mistakes, so maybe I can also on a few things."

Apparently Catherine, at first, felt at peace with Church teachings ("never crossing what the Church had said"), but eventually the knowledge acquired by experience and the knowledge handed down as Church doctrine came into conflict. She introduces qualifiers in her rhetoric ("I mean," "in my head") that may indicate an uncertain identification of need ("to delay motherhood") with the assumptions of her secular education ("unprepared women make inadequate mothers"). At this juncture, her struggle with the Catholic Church appears to illuminate a contradiction within the Church, its "mistakes on issues" and "good decisions." Her struggle seems to be a reflection of the actual state of "an institution" not always "on the ball." Catherine ends where she began, but on an entirely new plane: she sees both the Church and herself as fallible. She has relinquished both her original sense of the Church's inerrancy and her later sense that she had "made the right decision." She describes this new view of herself and her Church as the result of her having "matured."

Jacqueline's narration of her dealings with the Church over birth control differed. She approached her parish priest for help after her "first child was sickly and the second was just too much." After two more children, Jacqueline remained in her own terms "faithful, and I remember going to confession and telling the priest that I was having a very hard time with this."

Jacqueline found that, when she asked permission to use the rhythm method, the consent was limited. Her priest said, "Yes, but you can only do that for a couple of months. That's all I can give you permission for." At this point, Jacqueline sensed that the conflict was now between a woman and a man in authority who could not understand her condition. She asked herself rhetorically, but not her priest directly, "How could you say that to me? You don't know who I am. You don't know what's going on in my life." She decided, with her husband, to disobey: "We made the conscious decision then that I would not have any more children." This decision was a private one. "I have to tell you," she said, "I have told one other person in my whole life that I had my tubes tied, and I'm not proud of that for myself, but I feel comfortable in it because I had to make a choice and the choice was for my marriage. We couldn't live with more children, no matter how hard I tried."

For almost all of the women I interviewed in the Catholic community, birth control was the leading place of divergence between law and life—*Church* law and *their* life. Their responses to the cold unresponsiveness of the all-male priesthood were uniform in their dismissive vehemence:

> "How could you say that to me? You don't know who I am. You don't know what is going on in my life."

> "We don't have to listen to a man to say, 'This is right or wrong; this is what you have to do or don't have to do.'"

> "We feel when the pope has raised toddlers, we will listen."

Much less anger was occasioned by our discussions of abortion, where largely they were in agreement with the Church, though not necessarily with its rhetoric of child murder. Many of the women felt the Church had made a mistake and was even "foolish to lump that [birth control] with abortion." Sandra, for example, said: "I would separate the Church's view on birth control and the Church's views on abortion—like most [Catholics], we want it to be safe, legal, and wrong."

Catherine took a similar stance: "I would be uncomfortable in holding someone's hand during an abortion. I would be very honest in that." Although Lucy opposed abortion, she found that the way it was discussed in the Church did not take into account the complexity of the issue and said that it was for her a woman's problem: "I am not pro-abortion myself but I do find some of the conversation around it is so lacking in appreciation of the complexity of the experience . . . Only men could be so glib about the experience of women . . . I don't find them consistent. I think that if you're going to be prolife, you have to be prolife all the way down the line, not just in the womb."

By male inconsistency, Lucy meant the inconsistency of priests in condemning abortion while showing a relative lack of passion about the fate of unwanted babies carried to term and of their young unmarried mothers. The women I interviewed represented themselves as "prolife all the way down the line," by which they indicated their contempt for the American "prolife movement" whose members use aggressive and violent means in support of their "prolife" commitments and lose interest in life once a baby is born.

Marianne said of her own children that they "know we are anti-abortion," then added a qualification: "I don't know if I feel comfortable enough to say to them that this is absolutely, without question, dead wrong, and if you would even consider this, you would absolutely be sinning, or whatever." She then returned to her former stance: "Although they do know that we feel it's very wrong." And finally, she admitted to situations in her life that had in fact undermined her staunch faith in the position of the Church against abortion:

> I guess I know that it is very wrong, and I'm very much against it, and it's a very bad thing. But when I also was involved in foster care and saw some of these really, really poor, drug-addicted women having these children after children after children, and then society trying to take care of these children, and not being able to take care of them, and having them really going to bad places . . . I struggle and think, "Oh my gosh, I know that God would want us to say: 'Let's take care of these children.'" But the practicality . . . is anybody doing that? You know I don't know. And that's when I . . . that's where my heart takes over what is right or wrong, or what is my belief, or what is my staunch belief that I always felt was right or wrong. I don't know if I can be right or wrong with that.

Many of the women, Catholic and Jewish, spoke of a time in their youths when life and law were two neat packages and of a later period in their development when this bifurcation became less and less possible. Marianne obviously knows two conflicting truths—abortion is wrong; allowing children to go unwanted is wrong—and ends up asserting instead a lack of knowledge: "You know, I don't know." Yehudit described in detail how the clear distinctions of her early religious education gradually became blurred and frustratingly ambiguous:

> At one time in my ultrareligious period, when I went to Michlala, I was exposed to the world of intense Orthodoxy. There everything had meaning if the rabbis said so, and everything could be justified. Now, however, I am aware of situations where the human and the legal clash, and my general reaction is that the human is more important. This does not mean that the Halakhah should be set aside. I am very

far from that, but if you don't have the human or the healthy, then something is going on that can't be justified. Something is wrong. Whatever you do, you have to find a way to affirm the human, preferably (and that's putting it mildly) by not disregarding the Halakhah and by trying to hold the two together. But there must be a definite emphasis on human satisfaction when the issue comes up.

For instance, a religious music student at our Shabbat table described . . . feeling frustrated and deprived [because she could not perform artistically before men and women together], and I noticed that my reaction to her was a kind of double-bind feeling. There is something wrong if a talented young women can't express herself; that is not the way it should be. On the other hand, I feel the force of the Halakhah, and I try to say to myself: "Well, why doesn't she sing and compose for women?" But that is really not good enough for a woman seeking excellence—nor is it good occupational therapy! She wants to perform, and she feels she is talented. This is a situation in which I feel very frustrated.

Yehudit tried to maintain the perspective of an objective, dispassionate observer but gradually slipped into an empathic identification with one of the subjects. While she by no means would abandon the normative Halakhic framework, she admitted to siding increasingly with life as opposed to law: "It used to bother me when I was a child that a girl can't be a singer or a dancer. Theoretically, if I had a daughter who was tremendously talented in one of these areas, I think she would have to find a favorable ruling [from a rabbi to pursue these talents]. I think it might be possible."

In a similar context, Elisheva said: "I would be less hurt if my daughter ended up less religious, but she was fully 'present'—she was realizing all parts of herself." Elisheva thus expressed a preference for her daughter's happiness and self-realization over her religious conformity: "My daughter has a nonreligious boyfriend. I know that maybe I should be against it. I know what kind of problems can and will emerge, but I do not want her to give up her happiness."

Elisheva sets what she "wants" over and against what she "knows." Ideally, she would have liked her daughter Tali to fall in love with someone religious, but for Elisheva what mattered most was that her daughter be herself: "I don't want her to give up the Tali in her." It is not that she thought that Tali's life would be free of painful ambiguities. Her concern for Tali's happiness was informed by Elisheva's knowledge that life often involves discontinuity. She hoped for continuity, but not at the price of a daughter's life made unhappy by the demands of Halakhah. Elisheva, like Yehudit, were aware that law and life are sometimes at odds.

For Sima, a hard choice between life and law occurred not with respect to her daughter's life but in regard to her own hair. The Halakhah requires a married woman to cover most of her hair. This is not a private matter that can be hidden from public scrutiny. Sima had not initially realized that her decision to stop covering her hair would have repercussions for her daughter, who believed (and thought that others believed) that "mothers are supposed to cover their hair." Sima shared her reasons and her feelings with her daughter but could not reverse the powerful influence of the social ideal of the "good mother": "It bothered her very much. It disturbed her image of me as a *yiddishe mama* [Jewish mother] because all her friends' mothers covered their hair. As an adolescent, she believes that this is the rule, and that's it! How could there be such flexibility all of a sudden?"

Sima did not argue her case in the traditional way: she did not try to reinterpret the tradition or seek out a Halakhic loophole. Her mother had covered her hair, as had generations of women before her. Sima knew that she was flatly opposed to an accepted practice, one that she experienced as oppressive: "I simply told her that I personally can't take it anymore. Yes, it's true. It is the Halakhah, and even though I am aware of this, I just can't do it anymore. It bothers me so much."

Sima's candor and intensity were no match for the influence of the community's ideal type. "When she dresses up as a mother," Sima told me about her daughter, "she puts a kerchief on." "I guess," she continued, consoling herself that the issue in question is basically a matter of individual choice, "when she gets married, she will have to make her own decision."

For these women, mothering clearly cannot be separated from the culture in which they live, the particular religious culture that they are transmitting (cf. LeVine and Miller 1990). But as individuals they often find themselves resisting law and convention when they believe that they and especially their daughters would suffer psychological harm by strict adherence to religious teachings. Although their relationships with their daughters exist within a culture, their roles as mothers, in their view, extend beyond the boundaries delimited by their given normative tradition. They thus confront the most compelling of human dilemmas: it seems impossible to mother a child from within culture and impossible to socialize her from without. They struggle to maintain their own and their families' vitality within the constraints of their community. It is not, then, that a woman mothers either in a culture or in spite of culture, but that, since mothering consists of sets of relationships (between a mother and her children, a mother and her culture, a mother and her "self"), she relates to her children and to her maternal role within a dynamic context of commitments. Negotiating those commitments, beliefs, and attachments requires abdications and coalitions.

 *Teaching*

When mothers become teachers of other peoples' children, socialization ceases to be private. An aspect of family life becomes a visible component of a woman's public identity. One leading characterization of women teachers—as passive transmitters of norms and values in which they do not believe—can be discounted at the outset (see Dinnerstein 1976 and Herman and Lewis 1985). There is no credible evidence that their vocation as educators reduces women to pawns of the patriarchy, to automatons incapable of understanding the cultural traditions they have chosen to teach. Certainly this paradigm fails to describe or explain the lives of the women in this study, for whom teaching is a vocation more than a livelihood and who are critical and open-minded with respect to the cultural and religious traditions they are transmitting.

Nearly all the women thought that the schools in which they taught were settings where women's traditional roles could be significantly challenged. The Jewish women taught in institutions where women engaged in intellectual pursuits that were considered taboo a generation ago.[1] Until the beginning of the twentieth century, most women from traditional Jewish families either received no education at all or were educated in studies that had no bearing on religious thought or practice. Providing women with instruction in religious texts, such as the Bible and Talmud—the primary sources of rabbinic jurisprudence—is a relatively modern innovation (see El-Or 1994, 2002 and Heschel 1983). In the Catholic world, "it's only been the last forty or fifty years," Kathleen told me, "that theological education has been open—a theological degree from a Catholic university—has been open to women."

The women in this study, Jewish and Catholic, all agreed that their roles as educators go beyond responsibility for their students' intellectual development. All were actively engaged in questions of dress, prayer, and ritual observance, and even premarital sex. In discussing such matters with their pupils, they said they want to inculcate a spirit of intellectual honesty and curiosity and a readiness to question authority. In addition, they also want to instill a deep loyalty and dedication to religious law and tradition. Each had thought through the complexity of the multicultural world in which she had chosen to live, and each was articulate in describing the educational approaches that informed her teaching.

They spoke, in all, of three approaches available for different situations and contexts. The first approach focuses on the teacher as "educator" in the broadest sense of the term, as one who actively encourages her students to join the revolution to change women's status in religious law and tradition.

A second approach, which they all said they take in one form or another, is to teach girls to question and to think independently so that they can formulate (now or later in their lives) their own intellectual positions with regard to tradition.

A third approach addresses the need of adolescent girls to receive the clear and uncomplicated message that religious observance and faith are obligatory. The rationale behind this approach is that high school girls are not sufficiently mature to handle the complex religious issues with which their teachers struggle. This position was more evident in the women's decisions vis-à-vis their own daughters' education than in their interactions with their students. There was a discernible pattern in the way many of them adopted a more liberal philosophy of education with regard to their students than with regard to their daughters. The disparity between the progressive religious girls' schools where most of them taught and the more traditional schools to which they sent their daughters was a clear case in point. Yet even with their students, they felt they could not share their deepest questions but chose instead to express the "party line." They often argued that this was in their students' best interest.

Teaching Revolution

Miriam and Bruria feel they have a mission to capture the hearts and minds of their students in order to further a feminist transformation of the Jewish tradition. They believe that the emergence of a generation of highly educated religious women will leave the Orthodox community with little choice but to grant them equal status in Jewish law and practice. "Change will not come from the top downwards," Bruria insists. "It will only come if the community puts pressure on the rabbis." Elisheva shares Bruria's skepticism about the rabbinate ("To wait for them to change!"), and she also argues that change will occur if girls are educated to believe in and demand it. The ability and willingness to assume greater religious responsibility will change women's expectations of themselves, Bruria says, and this, in turn, will alter the status quo. The rabbinic authorities will feel compelled to make the system coincide *de jure* with the changes that have occurred *de facto*. The school is vital for providing the human resources necessary to wage the protracted struggle against the patriarchal bias of Orthodox Judaism. Girls should be taught to expect and demand their due from the system: "My job as an educator," Miriam says "is to give them a very clear message about self-fulfillment. The complexities and difficulties they can hear about elsewhere . . . I am aware that feminism does not attract all women and that Jewish feminism attracts proportionately even fewer women, but I would really like to see it happen in our school and with our graduates. If there is a small nucleus of women . . . then *something* will happen to the religious world."

Miriam is not naive, however, and realizes that her feminist values and goals are not shared by all of her colleagues: "Sometimes, in meetings, I overhear teachers from other schools saying things like they would like the girls to graduate and find appropriate matches for marriage. I begin then to ask myself whether *I* live in the real world or not."

But more disheartening than the lack of unanimity of purpose among colleagues is the lack of interest on the part of the students. As Bruria explains: "I would like to see the school become the vanguard of the revolution of religious women today. This, however, does not really interest the girls much. When I speak to them about it, our discussions remain very low-key. No one picks up the challenge of becoming active feminists today. These revolutions don't really interest the students."

Bruria, for instance, designed a course to show that feminist arguments are found in some traditional sources, only to discover that "this does not really interest the girls much." It is not that her students are discouraged by the difficulty of changing religious law; "it just doesn't interest them enough." Bruria supports this generalization by observing that her students often fail to extend feminist attitudes that they accept in their secular lives to their religious lives. "Many of them want to become lawyers," she says, "but none really want to be *dayyanot* [Halakhic jurists]." For them, the sexual revolution in the domain of religion is their teacher's agenda, not their own.

Questioning and Complexity

Another approach to teaching that these women talked about might be called Socratic: neither imparting knowledge nor attempting to socialize their students as full-fledged members of their communities, but challenging the unexamined, one-dimensional aspects of their students' worldviews. One of their goals, therefore, is to expose their students to the complexity of the religious tradition. As Miriam put it: "One of my jobs as a teacher is to show them the complexities of situations so that they shouldn't think just in terms of black and white. For example, take the Hellenistic period. I taught them that many of the high priests in the Temple became Hellenists, who, at the same time, continued to worship in the Temple. This was very hard for some of the girls to hear because it broke many of their preconceptions about Jewish history and the Temple."

It is interesting that Miriam's readiness to challenge the stability and simplicity of her students' beliefs about their sacred tradition stands in contrast to the way in which Miriam addressed the issue of "self-fulfillment." We have already heard her assert that her "job as an educator is to give [students] a very clear message about self-fulfillment. The complexities and difficulties they can hear about elsewhere." As a teacher, then, Miriam sees herself as having two distinct tasks, and these would seem to be contradictory. She wants to demonstrate complexity, to show that things are not "black and white," but she also wants to present a clear and unambiguous message. The difference is in subject matter. With regard to her students' potential as women, she is single-minded. She knows that they will hear all about the difficulties of being a modern woman from others, and, therefore, she sets as her task the presentation of a bright and uncomplicated picture of the opportunities available to them as girls approaching womanhood. With regard to their Jewish beliefs and convictions, however, she prefers to enter gray areas, since they have not yet been exposed to the complexity of faith and religious life. Miriam is willing to challenge what she considers simplistic views on Jewish history by emphasizing the all-too-human aspects of the past.

Miriam is aware of the painful process her students undergo when some of their cherished beliefs are challenged, and she does not relish the role of iconoclast as she once did: "It [the Hellenism of the high priests] was very hard for some of the girls to hear. It broke many of their previous conceptions about their history, the Temple, etc. Then, I was so excited to break their false preconceptions. Now, on the other hand, when I teach, it is not that I leave it out of the history lessons, it is just that I teach it with less enthusiasm, because I know the price of breaking innocence."

Miriam's initial excitement when offering her students the fruit of the Tree of Knowledge was tempered by her learning about the price of being expelled from the security of the Garden of Eden. While she believes in the importance of leaving innocence for the sake of knowledge, she no longer perceives it as a simple process without loss or pain.

Unlike Miriam or Bruria, Elisheva does not view her calling in revolutionary terms. She wants, more modestly, to see that her students are not being "brainwashed":

> The girls are being brainwashed by one position. We [the *bat mitzvah* program directors] will try to show that things are not that one-sided. There are many texts to choose from, and it is really a matter of choice. We will also show that many of the texts pertaining to women reflect specific cultural contexts. We want to show our students that, although some views are definitely found in the sources, there are other ways of looking at things. It is more complex than they think. We have evidence of times when women joined together and exerted pressure, and things actually changed.
>
> The world is in motion. It is not stagnant . . . I do not show only one side of things. I always show both sides . . . When I teach, I

always bring different texts pointing to different conclusions, and then let the students struggle with the differences. I bring Jewish texts and secular texts to show different points of view. I'm sure it will get me fired one of these days.

Elisheva does not seem to attach great importance to changing her students' behavior. While she does want to influence their minds, wants them to become "whole people," and knows precisely what she wants to give them, she also states that "what they do with it is up to them." From her point of view, they may well choose to follow the standard modes of behavior of the religious community—she only wants them to realize that there are other choices. Her criticism of most forms of religious education is that they present Judaism through a single lens, which, in her mind, is tantamount to brain-washing. High school girls should know about texts that describe women who actively participated in public community life, texts that were deliberately omitted from the traditional curriculum by supporters of a specific ideological attitude toward women and Jewish education. Furthermore, Elisheva wants to expose her students to texts from outside the religious tradition. She has little patience with the religious educational establishment, which sounds the alarm of secularization whenever its narrow parochialism is called in question. Although it was this tension that Elisheva had in mind when she said that she would surely be "fired one of these days," her comment was actually facetious and was immediately followed by "I know I am highly regarded as a teacher."

Elisheva does not feel threatened when advocating positions opposed to those of the institutions where she teaches. Her teaching vocation provides her, she says, with a way to express herself publicly. In spite of which, however, she still does not feel she is expressing herself fully. As she explained to me, "Tova, don't you notice how many women preface their thoughts with 'I am not really sure,' or 'I don't think I understood you correctly, but . . .'Baloney! They know very well what they mean and what the other person said!"

Having just listened to her description of how she speaks her mind as a teacher, I spontaneously responded to this assertion of reticence by telling Elisheva that what I heard was a very powerful and confident voice. She answered with laughter: "I guess I really do have a voice." As a teacher, Elisheva is clearly not intimidated. She, like Miriam, accepts the father's law as her standard of Orthodox practice, but the law that such teachers observe is a framework rather than a *diktat*. It is a cultural and religious context in which considerable freedom to maneuver and speak may be found.

Among the Catholic women, Kathleen seemed the most determined to get around the strictures set down by the Church hierarchy and teach her students to question. She said, in fact, that she felt her teaching gave her a good deal of power: "After a couple of years, I was able to influence the selection of religious texts and deal with the teachers in training. I was the one teaching them about ritual." In class, she claims she has two aims simultaneously: "on the one hand, to teach the traditions . . . but [the famous "but"] also to offer them and suggest to them that they need to ask questions. Always, always. That's always how I taught—that one needs to ask questions. I told my own children you always have to ask two questions, who says and why? So I might not have used that same language in teaching, but I would . . . try to elicit questions from them."

Ellen also claimed to teach her Catholic school students to question authority. I presented her with my notions of the three categories into which Jewish teachers might fall, and she aligned herself with the type of teacher that "opens questions."

"I think," she said, "that teenagers are really smarter than we give them credit for . . . We sell children way too short—way, way, way too short." Kathleen to some degree questioned the categories. She made a distinction between questioning and subversion. Asked to elaborate, she explained that "a questioner makes the person of whom they ask the question consider the answer. So that is all. It frames it. I think the person who asks the question helps frame the response. The one who questions is not the one who rebels, as the questioner asks of the teacher, of the tradition, to answer her question." Of course, Kathleen added, she was aware that questioning can lead to rebelliousness, but she held that a "questioner" is one that truly seeks answers and, in fact, forces the system and hierarchy to contend with her.

The ultimate authority of the Roman Catholic Church is its teaching authority, its claim to know and transmit inerrant truth from generation to generation and century to century. The Catholic hierarchy is very careful about exercising this authority over its schools, teachers, and pupils. This fact makes difficult the lot of the teacher whose aim is to encourage questioning. Kathleen recalled an interview with her bishop for a teaching job, an interview in which he compared the behavior he would expect from her to that of a soldier. She said that the bishop remarked that his own commanding officer in the military had said to him one time:

> "You can come in here, you can swear, you can shout, you can say anything you want, you can disagree with me. We can have the biggest argument you've ever had in your life. But when we go out there, it has to be a cheery 'Aye-aye, sir.'" And so he said [to Kathleen], "Not that I expect you to say 'Aye-aye, sir,' but we have to present a united front. We teach what the Church teaches. Can you do that?" I said: "Well, Bishop, I've been doing that all my life. Whatever I hold that might be my thoughts, might be somewhat different, doesn't make me less Catholic, but I would never assume to teach what is antithetical to what the Church teaches."

The bishop understood that Kathleen did not admire all doctrines and teachings, but he made clear that he was the address for her discontent. He did not want to silence her as an individual woman, only as a teacher of Catholic girls.

I reminded Kathleen of her liberal stance on homosexuality and asked whether she would teach that homosexuality was a sin. Her answer differed from the reply she reported giving to her bishop:

> No, what I would say when youngsters would ask me would be, "The church is still learning, because we're still growing. People are who they are, and we reverence a human being because God is present in that human being. And one person is not better than another person. A person just happens to be. The way a person expresses their life . . . they have responsibility for that. They choose to do good, or not to do good, and we cannot say objectively whether their actions are good or not good."

It would appear that Kathleen's only concession to the bishop and the magisterium of the Church was that she would not herself raise the question of homosexuality in canon law—but, if her students did so, she would speak of the Church as though it were a pupil: "The Church is still learning." Lucy also found herself walking a fine line between vocal disagreement with her superiors and conformity with the catechism. When one of her students was dismissed from school because she was pregnant, Lucy became indignant: "I didn't do this in front of the students but . . . to the administration. I think," she told them, "that this is un-Christian. I think this is not a tolerable policy or position, especially in view of the position you're also taking on abortion. I fought hard on that one, and we eventually changed the policy. But to the students, I would represent the administration's concern. But, without making a statement [to that effect], I think they knew that I was working hard to change it. I was always protective of them." Lucy realized, however, that "not everyone agreed with me that the classroom should be a safe place for people to speak their minds."

Catherine, in passing, made obvious why the clergy is so concerned that lay teachers not contradict the Church. Catholic school teachers, she told me, are taken seriously in the community and "have our own voice," a voice educationally more effective or at least more constant than that of the clergy: "Our priests rotate in and out of the parishes. So can he effect as much change when he only sees people once a week? Maybe he happens to see them once a weekend? You might only have him for a year or two, maybe longer. But I think as a teacher, at least within a school setting, seeing them five days a week, ten months out of the year, you do have more of a chance." Catholic school teachers, if Catherine is accurate in her assessment, seem well situated to bring about incremental, long-term change, at least in the attitudes of the laity toward Church doctrine and discipline.

A Clear Message

A third approach adopted by most of these teachers, at one time or another, is based on their belief that adolescents are not mature enough to deal with ambiguities. Expressions such as "adolescents need . . ." and "developmentally, girls at this age can't handle . . ." recurred frequently throughout our conversations. According to this common wisdom, ambiguities and nuances can wait until adulthood, when people can handle doubt without abandoning their religious and communal loyalties. But the common wisdom sounded odd coming from these women. None of them had expressed the slightest nostalgia for the innocence lost when the establishment is questioned. All appeared comfortable with their ambivalences, and none felt alien to her community or tradition. In their role of teacher, of formal socializer, the women chose to place the continuity of religious faith and observance first.

Rachel alluded to the psychological differences between adolescence and adulthood in making a distinction between the ambiguity that she could handle and the clarity that her students required. Even though she herself remained loyal to the tradition, despite ambivalences, she maintained that since adolescents think in terms of black and white, they are liable to abandon the tradition altogether if it is painted in shades of gray:

> It doesn't make sense to me, if I have certain questions, that I necessarily should share [them] or make someone else think about [them].
>
> I believe that high school education should be more or less directed.
>
> There is a big difference between what an adult and what an adolescent can handle. Theoretically, I think that pluralism is important. However, it is very difficult to teach pluralism during adolescence.

Rachel believes that her job as a teacher is to direct her students toward very clear goals and not to lead them to ask the questions she herself asks. While she does not question the value of pluralism, it is obvious to her that it is "very difficult to teach" to adolescents.

Bruria, too, was skeptical about which aspects of herself and of the tradition she could share with students. Her description of what they "can handle" stood in sharp contrast with the inner "peace" she says she has achieved with respect to the conflicting currents of her cultural and religious world:

> I am at peace with myself and with the fact that I cannot live constantly in harmony with all aspects of things. There are times when I lean towards one side, and there are times when I lean towards another.
>
> I do not think that at adolescence students can handle contradictory points of view.
>
> I think children need their naïveté. Criticism can wait until later. If criticism comes right away, something gets ruined.

Bruria's own exposure to complexity—her own loss of innocence—did not occur at high school, but only after many years of struggling with the system. She was thus certain that eventually her students (and her daughters) would ask their own questions. This psychological argument—that adolescents are not able to deal with uncertainty—conflicts with other positions these teachers hold. In other contexts, they would assert that the primary role of teaching is to elicit questions more than to answer them. Nevertheless, these women distinguished between sharing their own ambivalences with their students, on the one hand, and discussing controversial aspects of the texts and history, on the other. Even though they did not freely discuss their personal views with their students, they did not present them with a censored picture of the tradition.

Like the Jewish teachers, the Catholic teachers used "developmental appropriateness" as a gauge for determining what to share and not share with students. Catherine claimed that "not everybody is ready for that" when I raised the question of her teaching about her disagreement with Church policy on women's ordination. About the possibility of her teaching her complex stance on abortions, Lucy said: "I don't tell them everything I think about every issue. They are too young." The consciousness of what their students could handle, of the effects of teaching ambivalence to adolescents, was if anything more pressing to these women as mothers and socializers. "There will be a time," Seana said of giving her daughters a particularly controversial poem. "There are things I want to share with them, but it's a matter of timing and where they are developmentally." Ann began to share her critique of the Church when her daughter was older: "I wouldn't have shared as much about my dissatisfaction early on . . . but some of the value being integrated into the religion . . . [involves] putting away a lot of your own anger and dissatisfaction . . . I hoped to try to do it in conjunction with her ability for critical thinking—like Piaget stuff."

Lucy seemed to have found her own way of reconciling the first and second philosophies of teaching—questioning tradition versus transmitting it—though she described the balance as difficult to achieve:

> The challenge was to get them to think critically and to embrace their tradition. I hope I tried to model a person who loved the tradition and could be impassioned about it but at the same time who was thinking critically about the tradition and could tolerate their questions. I think that it is a very, very hard thing.

> The issue as a teacher was to encourage them to think critically and at the same time not jettison the whole tradition, and I don't think that's easy, especially for children or young people who don't think with a lot of nuance.

> One of the reasons I teach Scripture is because there is much more latitude there than there would be in teaching other things. I don't touch doctrine. So I don't wander into such tricky territory.

There was perhaps not so much difference in practice between Lucy's approach and that of the Jewish teachers, but her rhetoric evinced less ambivalence in her own life toward her religious tradition. Lucy "embraced," "loved," felt "impassioned" about Scripture, even if less so about Catholic doctrine, and strove to transmit her commitment and enthusiasm to her classes.

It might be said that Yehudit's insistence on an open and exhaustive analysis of texts as the most important factor in her teaching is a strategy not unlike Lucy's. Yehudit explicitly refrains from calling herself an "educator," preferring instead to be described as a "teacher of texts": "My mind seems to work in a completely different way [from conventional educators]. I respond to texts. Give me a text, and I'll respond to what I sense in it. I can prepare a class that integrates sources and connections between sources. I can sense connections between words. I feel that all I'm doing is guiding the reader, or the listener, through a narrative. I don't really have positions as I know other people do. It would be easier if I did. But then again, maybe not."

For Yehudit, since great texts are inherently complex, the process of teaching them necessarily involves ambiguity, questioning, and critical thinking. She cannot convey simple messages. Studying texts, she says, lends itself less to the formatting and enunciation of opinions than to something she calls "hovering."

Teachers Who Bring Their Teaching Home

The reluctance of some of the Jewish women I interviewed to refer to themselves as educators is indicative of a feeling that they were not fully present in their roles as teachers. Bruria, Shoshi, and Rachel claimed that the nature of the teacher-student relationship made it difficult to discuss their opinions with their students. Because contact between teacher and student is limited to the confines of the classroom and to a few hours a day, they felt they had to neutralize aspects of themselves. Shoshi contrasted her behavior at home and in class in terms of their relative "reality":

> I hope I am as good to my children as I am to my students. Teaching is very limited. It can almost be measured and looked at with a magnifying glass. I can count on my fingers times when I lost control of myself teaching. At home, however, things are more real.
>
> At home it is easier to be strict. In class you go in for an hour or two . . . Your words carry less weight. It is not as black and white as it is at home. In class I find that I neutralize myself more. I present myself the way I think I have to appear.

Shoshi's self-presentation in class filters out many of the spontaneous, real-life features of mothering. Bruria offered an interesting rationale for this filtering: "In school I do not allow myself to get angry, as I do at home. It is different being a teacher and a mother. At home, besides my being angry, they [my children] see how much I love them. In school, it is more difficult, so getting angry is more detrimental to them."

But, at least for Shoshi, school can also be an environment where the teacher feels "more real": "I find the school I teach in very positive. I don't feel that I have to hide myself or my ideas in school even if I do not necessarily agree with every single teacher. I think in work we can be more real because we can choose more or less where we work."

Apparently it is difficult to say whether home or school is "more real," and difficult to keep them as separate spheres. Shoshi, like many of the other women, said that she enjoys sharing her teaching with her daughter: "[My daughter] is a full partner in what goes on at school. She knows everything that goes on. She often asks whether she can help me grade papers or arrange school equipment. I talk to her about my teaching and also try out ideas for classes on her."

Moreover, the school context creates an important sense of detachment that enables mother and daughter to talk and interact within the safety of third-person discourse, where "they think" and "they should" take the place of "I think" and "you should"—a convenient way to discuss issues that are otherwise "too hot to handle."

Rachel fully understood the value of blurring the boundaries between her mothering and teaching environments:

> I like to share with [my daughters] things that go on in class, gossipy things and other things relevant to girls their age. Let me give you some of the background. My husband definitely hates my school. He thinks it is a very negative place, a place where there is no religion. When things go wrong there or I feel critical of the school, I hesitate to speak to him about it for it would only be an excuse for him to say: "I told you so." So often, when I want to share what goes on in school, I talk to the girls and not to him.
>
> I share with them my deliberations about whether to reprimand my students for not dressing modestly. There are certain girls who

come to school wearing miniskirts. I really don't know whether to raise this issue with the students or to ignore it. In my daughters' school they notice every little transgression and that bothers me too. I share these deliberations with my daughters.

Another extreme topic that arose in school was premarital sex. (If my husband were to hear about it, he would flip!) I don't think that independently of school I would have spoken to [my daughters] about it. This way it remained within the context of a school topic.

By speaking about what "they" say and what "they" do in school, Rachel and her daughters could discuss even premarital sex objectively without the usual inhibitions and emotional overtones—though Rachel clearly realized that they were dealing with more than just a "school topic."

Exceptions

Teaching girls seems basically to be a source of fulfillment and satisfaction. Although, as Shoshi often reiterated, there are times when she felt the need to neutralize a part of herself, the overall impression I received was that teaching remained an important vehicle for expressing personal convictions and values. Sima and Ann, however, were notable exceptions.

Sima underwent a crisis during which she felt hypocritical for teaching what she no longer believed in. Although she continued to be an outwardly observant Jew, she lost her sense of religious commitment and vitality. She therefore switched professions, leaving teaching for nursing. Her account of this change is illuminating, especially because it sheds light on the subjective, experiential aspects of teaching:

I stopped teaching because I stopped enjoying it. I liked having personal relationships with the students, but not teaching them. I no longer liked the intellectual side. And that is what I understood teaching to be about, certainly in the highly intellectual atmosphere of the school where I taught. I enjoyed the intellectual challenge to some extent, but when I stopped enjoying it, I went back to university and studied nursing. In nursing you really relate to other aspects of the person. It is really good for me.

Sima began by explaining her decision to change careers in terms of personal preference. At first, she had been drawn to the intellectual challenge of imparting knowledge. She enjoyed the excitement of teaching and the academic atmosphere. As time passed, however, she realized that her main satisfaction came from her personal relationships with her students. After realizing that this was not a passing phase, she made the decision to find an alternative career. Personal preference, however, is not sufficient to explain Sima's choice:

> I remember a teachers' meeting where one of the teachers commented to me: "You are so cynical." And all of a sudden I caught myself and thought, "Where am I in relation to the girls, to the other teachers, to the material I am supposed to teach, to the seriousness with which I should be teaching?"
>
> In other words, when you attempt to sell or pass on Jewish values in religious schools, there are lots of apologetics. For example, you try to prove that Shabbat [Sabbath] is something wonderful—even though you know that it is not necessarily the most wonderful thing in the world. You then have to distort your reality, or your inner feelings, or your own truth, in order to fit in with the values to which you want to educate. And I was really tired of this.
>
> In other words, at the time that it becomes clear to you or, I think, at the moment that it became clear to me, my identity or my position vis-à-vis religion, it was more difficult for me to lie. When it was still murky, you can do it, and it might even be that teaching contributed to clarifying some of these issues for me and brought me to this position that I can no longer do it.

Sima's language is most revealing. She first speaks in terms of her multiple relations. She is in relation to school, peers, children, students, and canonical texts. One might expect from her expansive list of relations that her relationship of her "relations" would be paratactic. (Paratactic syntax is a structure that relies on "and" connections rather than more complex ones.) Instead we find her using "or": "You then have to distort your reality, *or* your inner feelings, *or* your own truth, in order to fit in with the values to which you want to educate [emphasis added]." She experiences her relations as in conflict—so much in conflict that to keep them in balance she needs to lie—and so instead of "ands," she relies on "ors." She begins by referring to the problem of the conflicting values that teachers face in general, but then she changes pronouns, putting herself at the center of the narrative: "And *I* was really tired of this [emphasis added]." The impersonal "you" was replaced by the personal "I"/"me": "In other words, at the time that it becomes clear to you or, I think, at the moment it became clear to me *my* identity or *my* position vis-à-vis religion, it was more difficult for *me* to lie [emphasis added]." This switch parallels the psychological process that Sima undergoes before acknowledging her feelings and realizing that she can no longer continue as an educator at a school where she has to falsify her feelings in order to satisfy her peers, her students, and her tradition. Her impersonal analysis of what "*you* do" when "*you* want to educate" leads directly to her first-person conclusion: "*I* can no longer do it [emphasis added]." Sima felt she could no longer meet and balance in good faith the multiplicity of conflicting demands on the good enough teacher.

When I asked her to explain why she continued to raise her daughter in a religious environment and to send her to the very same school she herself had left behind, she replied: "I am not claiming that all of religious education is a lie. It's not all sanctimoniousness and a denial of reality. I don't want her to miss out on a religious education because that is the only way she will have a true choice when she is older. If you don't know anything about anything, then you don't have anything to choose from."

Sima rationalized her daughter's religious education in terms of her views about religious education in general rather than in terms of her personal experience. Religion is not all a lie, even if it did become a lie for Sima herself. She wanted her daughter to "know something" so that she, like Sima, could one day make a "true choice." What her daughter's choice will be seemed less important to Sima than its being "true."

One of the Catholic women, Ann, also left teaching, and, like Sima, not because of boredom with the job or from teacher burnout, but as the result of a complex interaction between her own intellectual and emotional development, on the one hand, and the patriarchal teachings she was expected to transmit, on the other. She said that honesty would require her to be critical of the Church— that "teaching Catholic girls first-year Scripture and morality was hard . . . I just didn't believe." She offered, as an example, that "you had to be married [even] if you didn't want to be" (i.e., a teacher could not be divorced). When I told her about Sima's experience, about her rationale for leaving her career as a teacher, Ann replied: "A lot of what she said is my experience. I understood that part [in Sima's transcript] about teaching the structures of the institution." It is, she said, "too difficult" as a woman to represent a male-dominated religion "in an official way," to be a spokesperson for aspects of the religion that she no longer accepted. Ann responded as well to Sima's decision to keep her daughter in a traditional religious school. Ann too wanted her daughter to have a religious base from which to make her own decisions.

My ambivalence was based on my age, experiences, and where I was at. I didn't want to impose that on her. I still pursue my faith, particularly in liturgy and Scripture study, and when I said something recently, based on that, Angela made a response that said she didn't know I was connected to that at all. I withdrew so much from her religious training, she doesn't know where I am! It generated a conversation. It is interesting that I feel very similar to what Sima is expressing.

While Sima and Ann remained part of their religious communities as women and as mothers, they were no longer willing to take responsibility for the socialization of other people's daughters. The rest of the women in this study have continued to educate and to pass on the law of tradition. They, on the whole, do not perceive this tradition as a foreign entity—the father's law—nor do they feel that they own the tradition completely. They define themselves in terms of their communities' traditions while continuing to articulate Western and feminist agendas. They do not feel their independence and autonomy as teachers betray the trust the community puts in them, and they agree to walk a fine line between conflicting cultural values and concerns. Sometimes they repeat views they are not at peace with because "that is all that adolescents can handle." But, considering the cases of Sima and Ann, that may be an equivocation. What they mean by "all that adolescents can handle," perhaps, is *all that they as teachers and mothers of adolescents can handle.* Once they, as Sima and Ann did, face the rift between their jobs as teachers and their own experience, they may well have no choice but to exit. The women who stay in the classroom say they are teaching in good faith—but not a good faith achieved by dissociation, disconnection, and capitulation. Many of the teachers might say that "good" is the wrong word. They might suggest adjectives such as "meaningful," "inherited," "secure," "familiar," and "familial."

CHAPTER FIVE

The Conflict of Dogmas

*M*any *of the women in this study have consciously tried* to unlearn much of what they absorbed in the religious homes of their childhoods and have had to struggle as well with the often contrary but equally dogmatic orthodoxies of Western psychology. Women expect to mother differently from the ways in which they were mothered, not only because of their unsatisfying experiences as daughters, but also because they are taught by the psychological oughts of their culture to want to be different kinds of mothers. While some of the psychological insights are helpful, many of the rules of "good enough mothering" can silence mothers, especially when these rules clash with other values or feelings. Subjective experiences of mothering often conflict with prevailing psychological theories about motherhood, and mothers often experience self-doubt, rather than question the received dogma.

Mothers do not experience their conflicts in a vacuum. They make difficult choices between competing ideals and values. None of the women I interviewed believed that she had resolved this difficult dilemma.

The Intergenerational Relationship

"When I think of my relationship with my daughter, I immediately think of a chain connecting my mother to me, and me to my daughter." Havva perceives her relationship to her daughter as part of an intergenerational chain that links mothers who are also daughters to daughters who are or may one day be mothers of daughters. The mothers I interviewed believed that their relationships with their daughters were informed by their early relationships with their own mothers.

"I'm really struggling a lot as a parent," Ellen told me. "My mother, she was just too busy . . . so for me to have this type of relationship with my girls, I have no base. I started babysitting and buying my own clothes in seventh grade. I couldn't stand what my mother bought for me any longer . . . And it's hard 'cause I tend to overdo things. It's things I never did with my mother, so I don't know how much is too much and how much is not enough." Clearly, what makes these seemingly straightforward activities critical is that they involve a break with the behavior and behavioral expectations of each mother's own mother.

Yehudit had consciously decided to disrupt the recurring intergenerational pattern by emphasizing the differences between her mother and herself. She made a point of mentioning to me how little she knew about her mother. Her mother, a Holocaust survivor, had so much to tell her, and Yehudit now wished she had paid more attention: "She had a very dramatic life . . . the Shoah, changing countries several times. She used to tell a lot of stories. That was great, but *you* forget. *I* wonder . . . *One* doesn't really see *one's* parents. The relationship is too fraught. *You* somehow don't see *your* mother as a hero of her own story but rather as *your* mother, someone sitting on top of *you* [emphasis added]."

Feeling a deep loss at not knowing her mother or her mother's story, Yehudit was determined that her daughter not experience a similar ignorance. She wanted her daughter to know her better than she herself knew her own mother. Yehudit desired to share with her daughter in a way that would enable memory. Confident that she could share so much more with her daughter than her mother shared with her, Yehudit was aware that her daughter did not know about many aspects of her life. Her public self, her teaching, and her social interactions were an integral part of her life about which her daughter knew too little. Havva's "unbreakable chain" thus reappears in Yehudit's story: "The fact is that I would like her to at least hear me once. This is necessary in order to know what I am about at all. After I'm gone, I would like her to remember something essential about me."

Yehudit feels her daughter's lack of knowledge most acutely because it recalls her own: "She may never really know me, as I never really knew my mother." She, therefore, is often overcome by feelings of wonderment over the positive aspects of her relationship with her daughter.

Marianne too wished that she would have known her mother better:

I think that if that kind of thing . . . from my Mom, that it would have been nice . . . that kind of thing that would kind of bond you as a woman, that kind of commonality thing, mostly about feelings and emotions . . . Some of the struggles that I go through I keep to myself because I don't feel that she may be able to lend what I need. It would have helped a lot of things and made the picture a little clearer—not like, "Okay, bye-bye now. You're married, and there you go. Clean your house, raise your children, and now you can cook." I never cooked in my life. I never ran a dishwasher. I never ran a washing machine. You know, my mother did all that . . . so it is just like by the decree of the wedding paper, marriage license, that now I . . . That's it. I knew that my mother . . . loved me greatly. And a lot of the rules and regulations that were in place were because of that. But I never heard that. I never heard that "this is the basis of what I'm trying to do and say to you." So I think that that is important.

Catherine was especially fearful of becoming a parent like her mother. She told me, almost in horror: "It's scary when you hear your mother coming out of your mouth, when you yell at your kids, and it's like, Oh my God! That was Mom." She described their problematic relationship: "My mother and I did not get along at all. Her favorite words when I was my daughter's age: 'You look like a slut. Don't do anything to embarrass me.' We just—we were as far apart as we could be." Catherine added that she now understands matters that could shed light on her mother. She sees her relationship with her daughters as the result of a conscious decision to do things differently: "Part of wanting to make sure I have a good relationship with my children is because I missed that."

Sima often catches herself relating to her daughter as her mother had related to her: "I can't believe sometimes the way I sound," she said. "I hear myself talking and screaming just like her."

The women continue to follow much of the same religious traditions as their mothers. In this sense, their lifestyles are similar. The Catholic women continue going to Church; the Jewish women follow the same yearly calendar of festivals, prepare Shabbat, and follow the same monthly menstrual bathing rituals, and so on. Yet this continuity is not enough to mask an underlying sense of discontinuity. The Jewish women, unlike their mothers, many of whom were immigrants to Israel, are Israelis like their daughters. They believe that the cultural gap between immigrant and native-born *(sabra)* generations is a significant factor in determining their self-images and their relationships. Similarly, the Catholic women experience a generation gap. They are all university-educated and working as teachers in Catholic institutions, unlike most of their mothers, who were full-time homemakers and had not had the opportunity to go to college.

The women I spoke with saw themselves in terms of a new social and historical reality that set them apart from their mothers, even when there seemed to be such similarity in religious practice. Elisheva claimed that her mother did not understand her world, neither now nor when she was a child. Bruria agreed: "My mother came from Europe. She did not understand where I was going on my class trips. She didn't understand the goings-on in my youth movement. I, however, was in the same youth movement as my daughter. We both were counselors. Although we did not go to the same high school, we both wrote the same state-required matriculations. She can share her thoughts about what to do in the army with me because I know what she's talking about." By their own accounting, it is this educational and sociological background that has enabled these women to have a closer, more intimate relationship with their children than they had with their parents.

Despite the importance of family in both the Jewish and Catholic traditions, most of the women felt that there was respect but no intimacy in their relationships with their mothers. They candidly described the emotionally unsatisfying nature of their relationships with their mothers without anger or bitterness. As they now understood it, respect and honor were not sufficient to fulfill their needs. These women did not talk about religious culture as a marginal concern, as if it were an artificial appendage to relationships. Common behavior patterns and religious cultural commitments were not enough to create the deeper bonds they missed. Although Elisheva's relationship with her mother was heavily influenced by the disparity between their worlds, she also articulated the disparity in their psychological styles and personalities:

> My mother never had a clue when I was coming or going, who I was with or what I was doing. Even if my friends came to our home, she was never in the picture. My relationship with my mother was problematic. There was no openness. She never shared her fears with me. My mother does not know what I do or why I get paid for doing what I do.
>
> I, on the other hand, go overboard and talk to Tali about things that I'm afraid she doesn't have the tools to deal with. She is still a child, but I think a channel has been opened between us. I hope it will stay open.

Despite Elisheva's awareness that she often exposes her daughter to too many of her fears and inner deliberations, she still insists on honesty and openness because of her commitment to a relationship in which they can be "real" with one another. "Being real" is crucial to Elisheva's understanding of mothering and of the relational framework she and her daughter share.

Kathleen spoke with equal candor about the different worlds she and her mother inhabited:

> I know she loved me dearly, but I also think she was also somewhat jealous of me, that I had the opportunity to go to college, that she had wanted but wasn't able to do so, that I was working and doing things because I wanted to do them, that she never felt that she could do [that] . . . She didn't want me to go very far from her.
>
> I consciously try to push my daughters in the sense of you find out what there is in life. Go experience the world in whatever way you can. Ask questions. Do things for yourself. Don't be afraid. My mother was afraid . . . I don't think she was ever the author of her own existence. And I think that's true of many women my mother's age . . . My mother was heroic in many ways, but these things I didn't want for my own daughters.

In a similar vein Ellen says: "I came from that type of environment where, you know, my mother was subservient . . . I do not want my girls to be that way at all. I just don't want that. I'm not as subservient."

Rachel was most reticent to disclose intimate details about herself and admitted to not "talking much" with her daughters. Yet when asked, she too emphasized the difference between her relationship with her daughters and the lack of intimacy with her mother. She claimed to know basically what went on in her daughters' lives, even if she did not know the details. ("It makes sense that they don't speak to me about certain things. They have their own friends.") An interesting parallel process emerged during the interview. At first, it seemed that Rachel would share very little with me about her relationship with her daughter: "I respect my daughter's privacy. It does not feel right to talk about certain things." She seemed to have a formal relationship with her daughter, sharing with her only what was "appropriate." As the interview progressed, however, and our conversation became informal, she began to share more. When I asked her whether her relationship to her daughter was similar to that with her mother, she offered a penetrating analysis of some of the main differences:

> My mother was a very concrete woman. She believed either you do or don't do something. I never knew that it was possible to have heart-to-heart talks. She never complained. She told us that we had to take responsibility for our decisions. To come to her and tell her we were sad or felt lonely . . . Who ever heard of such a thing! She would say: "You weren't asked out tonight, so do something else! Pick up a book and read." The whole feelings area was just not relevant.

Rachel's description of her *yekke* (formal) mother is summed up in her statement about the irrelevance of the "feelings area." Problems had to be "dealt with," not discussed. In sharp contrast, the "feelings area" was relevant and important to Rachel's relationship with her own daughter. They shared feelings and emotions but, as she noted, just "to a degree."

Havva said that she had consciously decided that her style of mothering would differ from what she had experienced as a child: "I was happy when we were together, either cooking in the kitchen or shopping, but there was a kind of steamroller feeling that we had better do things the way *she* wanted to do them."

Togetherness meant following her mother's rigid scripts about how to set the table, how to bake a pie, how to choose what clothes to wear, and what opinions to express. One of the central motifs in Havva's interview was her conscious decision to give her daughter enough room to express herself, even if this meant compromising some beliefs and withholding some judgments of her own. Havva worked hard at curtailing the use of maternal power to control her daughter and at silencing herself in order not to repeat her own mother's attempts to enforce conformity. Havva was also concerned about being more consistent than her mother, about not giving "double messages":

> I was very angry at her lack of consistency. There was always a double message. At first she would be on one side, then on the other, and then, if you agreed with her, she would again say the opposite. You know the Jewish mother joke: "Which do you like better, my gefilte fish or my chopped liver?" If you said the gefilte fish, she would say: "What's wrong with my chopped liver?" It was very much that kind of double-bind situation. One of the promises I made to myself was that as a mother I would be much more clear . . . There would be more honesty.

But these decisions and promises, this desire for a more extensive relationship with her own daughters, would later prove a source of frustration for Havva. When her children were young, these goals—

however difficult—were attainable. When Tami reached adolescence, however, things were no longer so clear-cut: "When you come into adolescence, things don't exactly come from the head; they come from the emotions." In spite of her good intentions and her commitment to consistency, the complexity of adolescence often left Havva in a quandary. She could not count anymore on her resoluteness and rationality to bring about perfect solutions: her reactions to difficult situations were not based exclusively on "reasons of the head." This realization made her feel helpless and confused because it showed that the intergenerational chain could not be broken simply by her being more self-aware and well-meaning. Her game plan for successful motherhood was in danger. In fact when children reach adolescence, mothers often discover a new and unsettling dimension to mothering.

Adolescence is somehow murky and tends to undermine the confidence of mothers. Erikson (1950, 1968) referred to this period of development as a "stage of identity crisis." As adolescent girls are challenged by the disconnections between societal prescriptions and their internal selves (Gilligan 1988, 1990a, b), mothers too are at a critical juncture at this time. Daughters and mothers undergo parallel processes. At precisely the moment when the patriarchy imposes its rules on an, until then, relatively free girl, it imposes on the mother the task of applying the rules on its behalf. During their daughters' adolescence, mothers begin realizing that the standards of good mothering they had set for themselves now seem more unattainable than ever. Despite Havva's good intentions and her confidence after earlier successes, she began noticing herself taking refuge in the very ambiguity and double messages she so desperately had tried to avoid. She felt frustrated by her own conflicting agendas. She recalls recoiling when her daughter entered the synagogue late, dressed in a little slinky black dress, which seemed to be her daughter's response to Havva's recommendation that she dress as she wished. It is not that there are necessarily more conflicts between mothers and daughters during adolescence, but those that do exist often constitute serious challenges to a mother's role and identity.

The Tyranny of the Shoulds and Conflict Avoidance

Many of the mothers who had put their faith in academia or in other sources of "objective" knowledge about mothering discovered during the turbulence of their daughters' adolescence that the "oughts" this knowledge prescribed did not always fit with their beliefs and feelings. In buying into the new religion of modernity and its gospel, its faith in good enough parenting, some of these women accepted norms and attitudes that became sources of discomfort and inner conflict. The knowledge lost its liberating quality, turning instead into a cultural straitjacket. The phrase "I should" was used repeatedly throughout the interviews. The context of should/shouldn't expressions usually revealed a clash between idealized expectations and real feelings. "I know I shouldn't have cared so much when my daughter told me to leave the circle because she preferred to dance with her friends," admits Shoshi, "but I really did!" Subjective experience is thus measured against normative ideals of motherhood; there is a right way to feel.

Because these women are at the crossroads of at least two cultures, they are negotiating several sets of imperatives about the right way to behave and feel. In addition to their traditional commitments as Jews and Catholics, they have accepted the codes of proper mothering dictated by Western psychological traditions (see Erikson 1950; Caplan 1989).[1] This multiple commitment is made still more complex by the determination of these women to be different from their own mothers, a motive that doesn't always overlap with either of the other two. The disparity between "ought" and "is"—between *theories* about motherhood and the *experience* of mothering—leads to feelings of guilt and self-reproach and eventually to the silencing of aspects of mother-daughter relationships that reveal this disparity.

The conflict between motherhood and mothering was expressed in a variety of should/shouldn't statements:[2]

> "I know I shouldn't care so much what my daughter chooses to be, but I do."

> "I know I shouldn't be so proud of my daughter for being chosen to be in the accelerated math program, but it really makes me proud."

> "I know I shouldn't get angry about those silly things, but I do. I try to hide it and not show her how much I really care."

> "I know I shouldn't have such agendas for my children . . . I don't like that part in me."

> "I know I shouldn't care so much that my daughter chose to go to a different high school from the one in which I teach."

> "It disappoints me that I had these dreams for her, but then what can I do?"

> "I should be happy that she is growing up, but I am afraid I will miss her so much when she goes into the army."

> "I should be happy that she loves her teacher so much and confides in her. I should be happy that she is able to have relationships with other adults . . . but I feel jealous. Of course, I don't say anything to her."

> "One time she was not accepted into a course. She was really withdrawn, and she cried, but she did not want me to comfort her. She called her friend who came over. That upset me tremendously. I was very immature."

"I know I shouldn't dress this way because it embarrasses my daughter."

"It is very important for me that my son study Talmud, but I do not feel that way about my daughter. I know I shouldn't, and it goes against what I thought I believed in, but this whole issue arouses primordial reactions that are just there."

"You have this obligation to teach your children to be social beings."

"For the sake of comfort for others, I backed down."

"I didn't want to cause scandals for my daughters."

The normative ideal of motherhood that inspires such expressions of self-criticism is that of selflessness. Notwithstanding the modern emphasis on self-expression and authenticity, a mother is expected not to have her own agenda for her children or to express her messier feelings toward them. She should not be bothered by their refusal to help with the housework. She should not feel hurt by her daughters' rejection or indifference, nor should she take pride vicariously in their achievements. Her *raison d'être* is to facilitate her children's growth. Being conscious of and expressing her own needs and even having such feelings are signs of selfishness, immaturity, possessiveness, overattachment, and neurosis.

Because these "oughts" and "shouldn'ts" often conflict with what women really feel, mothers may choose to silence a part of themselves for the sake of being "good enough." The tyranny of the "shoulds" can thus produce self-alienation or paralysis and undermine genuine relationships. Although modern women have been granted permission to speak up as professionals, for example, as mothers they are still expected to show restraint and not violate sacred "prohibitions against female anger" (Herman and Lewis 1989;

Kaplan 1992). The absence of overt conflict during adolescence can be explained without resorting to Freudian notions of neurosis or to idealized conceptions of harmony: adolescent girls may silence themselves in order to protect their mothers from becoming *"nervous chalerias."*[3]

Little conflict was reported in my interviews. This was not only the result of parent-child affinities, whether personal or cultural, but also reflected the combined efforts of mothers and daughters to suppress various needs in order to remain good enough. It is as if women and girls were being trained, as previous generations indeed were, to prefer silence rather than risk conflict: "I often silence myself. I ask myself: 'Is it worth it, over this, to have a fight?' It is often better to keep quiet than to engage in conflict."[4]

Here Elisheva remarks that she often chooses to conceal what is on her mind when this would facilitate Tali's feelings of closeness toward her. Elisheva does not, she adds, want to be a "walking commentary." She is convinced that expressing her needs not only can produce conflict, but also can be oppressive and psychologically harmful to her daughter's development. Yehudit feels much the same and wants to protect her daughter from dangerous parts of herself: "If there is one thing I am afraid of, it is of oppressing her . . . I keep back many times in order not to oppress her."

Conflict is avoided by pacts of silence. Daughters "agree" to treat their mothers as good mothers; mothers "agree" to treat their daughters as good daughters. When Shoshi's daughter told her, for example, that she preferred dancing with her friends, Shoshi withheld expressing feelings of hurt that she believed reflected a "pathological" side to their relationship. Again, Miriam's daughter was encouraging and supportive of her mother, despite the fact that her mother often came home late and so was not "there" for her. Miriam knew about her daughter's protectiveness and about her reticence to express her need for a more available mother. She is *"too* good and *too* thoughtful," Miriam said, then added: "This hurts me very much because I guess I cause her to say things that she does not believe in." By the judicious use of silence, mothers and daughters protect each other and their good enough relationship.

Conflict Resolution

With several of the women I had more than one interview. At the beginning of the second interview, I asked each whether she would like to add or clarify anything with regard to our previous conversation. Most drew my attention to what little mother-daughter conflict they expressed in the previous interview and were interested in explaining how things had changed in a positive way. I was told that the conflicts in question were temporary aberrations that could be dealt with and ultimately resolved. It was as if the relationships of the mothers and daughters had changed for the better during the six-month period between the first and second interviews. At first this situation puzzled me, especially since this "change for the better" had occurred for the majority of the women at precisely the same time. Perhaps the transcripts of the interviews created discomfort—the women may have been disturbed by the sense of unchanging permanence that written documents often produce. Some may have felt a need to "correct" the written record by emphasizing the fluidity of their relationships. I wondered whether it was difficult to stay in the presence of conflict, where the cultural pressures to agree and the "ought" of good mothering meant no conflict with one's daughters. Also, although the women were honest and candid and quite willing to share their personal stories with me, I wondered whether I had come to represent the voice of dogma, ready to shun these women for having conflicts with their daughters. Was I regarded as an outsider and potential critic? Since the basic method of this study is to listen to women's voices without speaking over them, I am hesitant to question these striking coincidences.

It is of course not inconceivable that these problems were in fact resolved. Havva said that she and her daughter Tami were beginning to talk to each other about Tami's future without anxiety or tension. During the first interview, Sima spoke about how hurt she had been when her daughter developed a close relationship with her homeroom teacher. She confided in her teacher about matters she would not tell her own mother, even including discussing her conflicts with her parents. During the second interview, I was told that "things with Maya have straightened out. She knows she has parents, and if anything comes up, she tells us first."

The most dramatic change involved Sara and her daughter Hadas. Initially, Sara focused on her own feelings of rejection and loss resulting from a crisis in their relationship. Sara moved from their small community to Tel Aviv to spend a sabbatical year, so that her daughter could celebrate her *bat mitzvah* in a meaningful way. Despite Sara's good intentions, the move proved to be disastrous for Hadas. She had a hard time adjusting to school and making new friends, and she became difficult and irritable. A major part of our first interview revolved around this problem: "Because of what happened these past couple of months, my daughter left Tel Aviv and went back home to Nevei Galim. This is very difficult for me, in part because of my realizing how easy it was for this to happen. I mean, life goes on even though something abnormal has happened. I keep thinking: 'How did I get into this situation in *my* family? How could this happen to *me* . . . How could *my* daughter do something like this at such a young age?'" Sara was fully awake to the depth of the crisis, noting that, although she spoke to Hadas every day, most of these conversations were "typical phone conversations."

Sara had not consulted with her children before making her decision to live in Tel Aviv but had simply presented it to them as a *fait accompli*. Hadas defied her parents' expectations and fought with them and with her teachers. She convinced the gym teacher to allow her to wear a skirt (for reasons of religious modesty) and insisted on praying with the older girls because "the atmosphere was more serious." The situation at home was no less turbulent. She complained about everything and was visibly unhappy most of the time. After a few months, Sara realized that the situation would not change and that there was no point in trying to force her to stay in Tel Aviv. Besides the obvious fact of her daughter's suffering, she herself could no longer bear the incessant arguments and confrontations. Consequently, she allowed Hadas to return to Nevei Galim where she lived with relatives. Hadas returned to Tel Aviv every two weeks to spend Shabbat with her family. Sara expressed mixed feelings about her daughter's fighting spirit. On the one hand, it bothered and upset her because it was a sign of a general "nagging personality," which in her words "drives me crazy":

> The classical issues of adolescence started in her case at such a young age. It is just amazing. Every five minutes she would remember that she needed something. One day I would take her to buy knee socks (she always covers her legs), then the next day she would remember that she needed hair clips. To hell with it! I finally have some free time to devote to her . . . She drives me crazy. I come home exhausted from work, and what do I hear the minute I open the door? My daughter complaining or nagging about something. Either she needs something, or she has to argue about something.

Nevertheless, Sara also appreciated the positive side of her daughter's resoluteness. The same behavior and personality trait that caused Sara so much frustration and pain also caused her to feel pride and admiration. She was genuinely amazed and impressed by her daughter's decision to pack up and leave and by her unwavering conviction that she knew precisely what she wanted and needed: "On the one hand, I say 'Hats off!' to my daughter. How I admire her! What strength she has to fight for what she needs and at such a young age! On the other hand, it makes me crazy. She just does what she wants to do! But then, I also do what I want to do . . . Why be surprised? . . . But nothing with her was ever easy."

Sara recognized herself in her daughter's courageous and independent spirit. After all, Sara had all alone challenged the religious establishment in Israel many times. She had always been politically active and figured prominently in many public debates. She identified herself and established a well-deserved reputation as an "Orthodox feminist."

However, seeing herself in her daughter was not only a cause for gratification but also a source of complex feelings of guilt and self-reproach. While she understood and empathized with many aspects of her daughter's personality, she was angered and embarrassed by others. For Sara, Hadas served as a mirror of herself to such an extent that Hadas's behavior also revealed aspects of herself she preferred to ignore: "There is something else in her personality that disturbs me because I think she inherited it from me . . . When I look at her when she upsets me, I ask myself: 'What am I seeing?' Perhaps I am seeing what upsets me about myself. When I look at the boys, I usually see what I love about my husband. But when I look at her, I see what disgusts me about myself. This disturbs me. I don't understand it."

Throughout the interview, Sara repeatedly spoke of her feelings of frustration, which grew more acute as Hadas reached adolescence. Sara apparently lost confidence in her ability to mother and to deal effectively with her daughter's needs. Nothing she did was good enough for Hadas:

If I interfere, it is not good. If I don't interfere, it is not good. If I clean her room, it is not good. If I don't clean her room, it is not good. If I try to hug her, she rejects me, but if I leave her alone she feels rejected . . . The boys love to be hugged and kissed.

It is impossible to kiss her. She doesn't let me come close. She is not gentle. I am sure that she needs love, and it bothers me that I haven't found a way . . . except when she is in trouble or in pain. Then one can hug her and kiss her. I don't really know what she wants. I don't know what she needs. Maybe she needs a mother who is home all day cleaning up her room and making her whipped cream cakes.

It is not clear what she wants from me, and it is not clear what I want her to want from me. This just strengthens my nervousness. I don't understand where I am or what am I doing here as a mother.

Hadas was not very cooperative with her mother, and Sara was not prepared to hide her frustrations behind a mask of noble self-denial. Unlike the mother-daughter dyads discussed earlier, this relationship involved little self-silencing by either partner. The only resolution that either could conceive of was separation: "One of the things I feel guilty about," Sara said, "is that my life is so much simpler since she left."

The relationship between Sara and Hadas underwent a radical change a couple of months later when the whole family returned home to their *moshav* (small collective community). Sara's lifestyle began to change so that she spent much more time with her family at home. Her second interview is a personal account of rediscovering her relationship with her daughter:

I had to change my lifestyle so that my relationships would change. In this sense I am a Marxist. I decided to become a "small head" [to keep a low profile]. Although I continue to work, I only teach at the local high school—a less creative job than what I was used to. I shall not take on new projects or engage in politics. Instead, I am going to organize myself, my home, and my children in a new way. This is what really interests me now.

The difference in my life has influenced Hadas most because she is very good at taking advantage of my free time. She grabs hold of me now. I am constantly amazed. She is a new person. I often ask myself whether other parents believe that their children change so much, so quickly. It warms my heart so much.

We had a very difficult time for about half a year (it seemed so much longer then). Now she is an adult at home. She still has her *shtick,* and I still sometimes yell at her to clean up her room. But this is rare. Now our negotiations are between adults. I now ask her whether she *can* . . . I take her plans into account. I cannot take for granted that she will do everything that I ask of her. After all, she has a life of her own. She can explain to me why she cannot do this or that . . .

She helps so much more in the house. She does things because she really identifies with her home. I am surprised at how well she is arranging her life. She started to play piano again. She may not practice the way a bourgeois girl practices, but she has her own standards of playing, and I respect that (even though her teacher is disappointed). This is exactly how I behaved. I chose the scores that I liked, and I played them. This is exactly what she does. It astounds me how similar we are. She is more like me than I imagined. She plays the same piano that I did, and if I close my eyes, I can see myself in our little apartment in Bayit Ve-Gan.

Whereas in the past seeing herself in her daughter made Sara feel frustration, estrangement, and even disgust, now the experience awakens feelings of closeness. Sara is truly amazed at the extent of Hadas's change in the course of a year:

As a child she never drew a single picture in kindergarten. I was always embarrassed. My friends' refrigerator doors were covered with their children's drawings. But this year, all of a sudden, she started drawing. She taught herself by using the Russian system of copying. She worked as a baby-sitter, and with the money she earned, she bought a calligraphy set. She is teaching herself artistic writing. She used to make so many spelling mistakes, which drove me crazy! Now she gave me as a present a Naomi Shemer song, which she transcribed beautifully. The song she chose was "Every Blade of Grass Has Its Own Melody."

I am very proud of her for choosing not what her parents tell her to choose, but what she likes and what is meaningful to her. She works hard at her piano playing and often asks me for help with songs she composes! She asks me! She comes to me with questions about little things because she thinks that I can help her!

She has learned to take care of her hair. When she was a little girl, I had to remind her to brush her hair. She always had knots, and so we kept her hair short. My mother would tell me how disappointed she was that her granddaughter didn't look like "a little doll." It has to be brushed after washing and then left alone. It looks simply marvelous. I had no idea! She found this out from her friends, from her peer group. And she is so right! I never thought that she was a pretty girl, but she really is! She found out what to do to be pretty. She also found out what type of clothes make her look good. I should learn from her.

Her teacher mentioned how much Hadas admired me. Hadas's class had to write about influential women in their lives and explain their choices. Hadas wrote about her mother and gave as one of her reasons "because she is very smart and respects different kinds of people." (Of course she did not tell me this. I had to hear it from her teacher.) I was so moved and happy that she mentioned the very things that I wanted her to know about me.

When she reflected on some of her past life decisions, Sara interpreted many of them as rebellions against her own mother and the "establishment." Then, she felt liberated from the shackles of having to be the "perfect girl." Now, however, she thinks that she may have lost control of her life. She no longer believes that what she did then necessarily reflected her real needs. Her political and public activities no longer fully express what she wants for herself today. She thus has chosen something different and wants to be respected for it:

I decided to finish my adolescence now, to end my rebellion against the world and to come home. When I started living the way I wanted—which was very different from the orderly way of life my mother wanted—I entered into a whirlwind which I could not control. I did things not necessarily because I wanted to, but because I couldn't stand being the kind of person who didn't do those things. I never really asked myself, "What do I really want?"

Now I want quiet. I want a clean, calm, and orderly home. I want an aesthetic home, nice food, nobody to bother me . . . Everyone says that I will eventually enter politics again and that this is just a phase. Well, meanwhile it is what I want, and it is a good thing for me and my family.

Gaining Voice—Losing Voice

Sara's parting comment to me at the first interview—"I want to be a mother and not a woman for her"—was perhaps a premonition of the dramatic change she would undergo during the next few months. Sara's second interview could be described as a personal disclosure of her rediscovery of motherhood and of her new ability to break down the barriers of self-consciousness that had blocked her from perceiving her daughter as an admirable person deserving of respect and interest in her own right. Whereas in the past, Sara had felt that her convictions and beliefs were sufficient for making decisions for her children, she now realizes that if she wants something from—or for—Hadas she must ask first.

The question remains, however, whether Sara had to sacrifice being "a real woman" in order to become "a good mother." In other words, one can read this second interview in terms of loss rather than of gain. Sara chose to give up part of her former identity in order to have a relationship with her daughter. Her reference to a "Marxist" interpretation of her personal history and past was meant to suggest that in order for her relationships to change, the fundamental structure of her lived reality had to change. Sara understood that she could not alter the psychology of her relationship with Hadas without first changing certain elements of the basic framework of her life. Sara, the political-religious activist par excellence and a symbol of the new women's voice in the Orthodox community, decided that she was tired and needed a rest, but, more important, that she had to give her relationship with her daughter a second chance.

Another example of this kind of interplay between loss and gain was Havva's choice to go back to university and study creative writing when her daughter was still a baby. She now believes that this career choice cost her a great deal in terms of her relationship with her daughter. Yet she feels that she had "no choice." She "had" to develop this aspect of herself because she was "choking." She needed to discover another form of self-expression in addition to mothering and to teaching. Once again, on the surface, Havva's appeared to be a success story. She resisted the patriarchy and actively challenged many established conventions and institutions. Aside from successfully changing careers, she helped build a synagogue and an elementary school. Her actions were not confined to an underground but were instrumental in bringing a new public order to the traditional social and religious frameworks in which she lived. Today, however, she has misgivings about some of these accomplishments. She is aware that in making choices she has suffered losses in spite of all her gains. She realizes that the consequences of choice cannot always be controlled or predicted. Gain and loss are more closely connected than she had originally thought.

Sara's story elicited in Kathleen memories of her own struggle, a struggle so eloquently described that the narrative is worth quoting at length:

> When I heard about Sara, I thought that there should not be a discrepancy between being a "mother" and a "woman"—there must be a way to be both. Sometimes I think that I have achieved that, but your interviews give me pause. When I had first graduated from college, I had wanted to continue my education in theology, but there was not much available to Catholic women at that time. And because I was not a member of a religious order—a nun—no one whom I knew thought that it would make any sense for me to pursue theology. And it just seemed like a dream to me, not something that an ordinary woman in the Catholic Church would or could do.
>
> When our third daughter was almost three, our pastor asked me if I would give up my job in the local public school system and come to

work full time for the church as director of religious education. It meant giving up money and benefits, but it seemed like an opportunity to connect with my younger dreams. In the first three months of my work, I knew that I needed to get a master's degree in religion/religious studies if I were to continue. There was a need to validate the work and honor the people that it served, as well as support me in my quest to develop a curriculum that was pedagogically and theologically sound. When I approached the pastor about continuing my education, he said to me, "But, Kathleen, we like you just the way you are." He did not offer to help with the tuition—if I wanted to go, I was on my own. I applied to Notre Dame and began my pursuit of my degree. I could only do one course at a time. Neither my husband, my mother, nor my pastor thought that it was necessary, but no one deliberately stood in my way. It meant juggling the world again, but this time I was determined, for my own sake, to pursue to the end.

Nine credits into my studies I became pregnant with our son. My mother developed a slow-growing untreatable cancer and what I realized in retrospect the first signs of Alzheimer's disease. I took a semester's leave of absence from Notre Dame. After Alex was born, I returned to school, this time continuing to work and continuing to care for all of the people that needed to be cared for. I wanted to do this so passionately that I did not care how exhausted I became. It was during my studies at Notre Dame that I fully came to understand and articulate my own theology. I loved my studies—and I was good. I learned that I was a natural preacher, that my voice added to the world in a way that was important. If I had had fewer responsibilities, if I could have permitted myself the leeway, I would have done more. As it was, it took me almost five years to finish my course work and then another three to finish my comprehensives/thesis. But when I did finish and took my orals, I passed with distinction.

Because of the needs of my children and my mother, I did have to put my studies on hold. My daughters—my children's—lives were moving so quickly, my mother's illness was so awful that I needed to be present in ways that meant I had to give up the dream that was mine. I never really used my voice in the way that I might have . . . I do know that my choices in life, my ability to affect the world around me, have been greatly shaped by my need and responsibility to be the mother, the caretaker, the one who does for others.

I believe that each of us has something to accomplish in life—something that no one else will do. In your interviews, Miriam's concerns about competing goods of self-expression and availability to family and friends hit home with me. I still ask myself the question: Why is it that women have this conflict? My friend physically and economically supported her husband and raised two children while he pursued a doctoral degree. They had a social life and a lovely home—so long as she provided it. Is that what she was supposed to accomplish in life? She is a brilliant woman, who, if she had become an economist, might have had far-reaching effects [and] the world might be a better place. She has wonderful children, but they are not her. They do not have the same insights, not the same interests.

My children are the joy of my life—but they are not me. What I might have accomplished if I had studied, written, argued, taught, might have added to the understanding of a God of great diversity. Perhaps my voice might have helped to move the world a little closer to acceptance of all the created universe as equal. Maybe, also, these are delusions of grandeur! I have done what I could do—what I could give myself permission to do. I do believe that claiming voice above ground has a rippling effect that spreads beyond our individual lives, and it is costly. But silence is more costly. Silence chokes the one who is silent and permits evil to flourish. Silence allows a cacophony because the harmonizing voice or the descant voice or the lead voice or the solo voice is absent.

Kathleen's story has a coda. "I loved my girls," she told me, "and loved being with them. I really do not think that they suffered because of my trying to do more." And yet, she related the following:

When our second daughter was applying to college, she was very angry with me because I insisted that she apply to at least one women's college. She did not think that that was necessary . . . Sally accused me of trying to force her to live my life, or at least a life that I would like to have led. She accused me of being resentful of my children and my family, and feeling as though I had not accomplished what I wanted. According to Sally, I was resentful of men. Well, she was going to live her own life. I was stunned. I did not think that I had exuded these feelings. I had worked so hard to be everything to everyone, except myself. She saw something that I had not even known was there to see.

I told her at the time that I did not resent my children. They were the best things in my life. Just because I was a feminist did not make me resentful of men. I was resentful of the sense of entitlement and the lack of respect for diversity. I was furious at the way women were dismissed still. The only reason life was in any way better for me than it had been for my mother was because of my education. I wanted [my daughter] to have more opportunities than I did. I did not realize that she felt hurt by my life in some way.

She chose her own school . . . and graduated with honors from law school last year. Yesterday was my birthday. Sally gave me a card that said: "Mom, when I think about how I want my life to turn out, it always comes down to 'I want to be just like you.' No one has ever had a better example in life than I have had in you." I have not stopped crying yet.

Kathleen experienced her daughter's accurate appraisal of her mother's resentment of her self-sacrifice on her family's behalf as an accusation. What startled Kathleen was her emotional transparency: how could her daughter think that she was resentful, when she had "worked so hard to be everything to everyone"? And the question remains—given that Sally's choices were made in spite of her mother's desires—what is the content of Sally's birthday blessing "I want to be just like you"? Which "you," or which part of Kathleen, does she see and want to emulate?

The mothers I interviewed learned the hard way about the scarcity principle: time and energy are finite resources that have to be carefully balanced in order to minimize the human costs of our choices.

"I hope that what I am doing outside of the home will also be a model for my daughter"—Miriam was relieved that her daughter did not complain about her unavailability, but she worried that her daughter might be suppressing her feelings for her mother's sake. In other words, Miriam was afraid that the price of her gaining voice was her daughter's losing her own. This conflict between the competing goods of self-expression and availability to family recurred throughout the interviews. Sara and Havva tried to resolve the dilemma each in her own way, Sara by returning to more traditional mothering, leaving behind her more political pursuits, and Havva, by going back to school, leaving much parenting to her husband. Elisheva blamed her predicament on her generation's delayed appreciation of a mother's need for self-fulfillment, independent of her role as mother. Elisheva expressed hope, however, that things would be different for her daughter:

> I see myself as a member of the desert generation that has not yet entered Canaan.[5] I am a product of a traditional community, of a society that educated boys and girls differently. I am a product of my culture. I could artificially change but I refrain from doing so. I represent not only myself but a whole generation that was taught to believe that women are not complete.
>
> Theoretically, I have both feet in the new world. I know from my own experience, however, that I am not able to make the transition. I am a product of a certain socialization. Can I, all of a sudden, at the age of forty, erase it all? The price may be too great. So I don't even try.

Elisheva understands the difference between intellectually knowing about freedom and being psychologically capable of internalizing what is in "the head." She hopes her daughter will be better prepared to make the leap than she was. She therefore is bringing her up in a way that will make her entry into "the promised land" as peaceful and natural as possible.

Rachel too believes that her daughter's development will be easier than her own. She has no illusions about the differences between the two of them but hopes that her daughter will complete her studies and develop an appreciation of her own individual needs before getting married.

Havva explicitly says: "I want my daughter to be better than I. I don't want her to make the mistakes that I made." This deep desire is a source of conflict between them, especially when Havva realizes that Tami may not be able to do better than her mother, despite all efforts. She does not want Tami to go into the helping professions, which, she believes, drained her of so much of her own creativity. Havva believes that the price of her not attending to her own needs earlier was her not caring for her daughter in the way that she would have liked. She relinquished this aspect of their relationship to her husband who took over caring for Tami at an early age and who now has a closer relationship with her. Havva regrets her loss of intimacy with Tami: "There isn't the one-on-one time that I would like to have with her." Havva believes that she sacrificed an important aspect of her connection to her daughter by choosing to be herself. She hopes, however, that her daughter will be able to achieve the balance that proved to be so difficult for women of her generation.

Claiming or reclaiming voice does not occur in a vacuum nor does it take place underground. When women claim voice above ground, there is "a rippling effect that spreads beyond their individual lives" into their immediate and extended environments. Self-expression may be unexpectedly costly. Losses seem invariably to accompany gains. They may be distinguished in theory, but in practice, they are often inseparable.

"No Perfect Places"

The position and positioning, the self-placement be-
tween modernity and tradition, between family and self-fulfillment,
between commitment and resistance lend support to a fluid model of
mothering. Identifying a "community" voice, a "religious" voice, a
"resister" voice, and an "inner" versus an "outer" voice has been use-
ful in identifying points of conflict between the community and the
individual, but in this study these voices are internal or have been
internalized to various degrees by the mothers I interviewed.[1] Their
many voices are influenced by their communities, families, profes-
sional colleagues, religious leaders, and other factors that one may
term "external," and no one of these voices can lay claim to being the
women's authentic or dominant expression. But these women feel a
genuine and painful ambivalence or multivalence. Not only are these
women raising daughters and teaching girls in orthodox cultures,
they have consciously and deliberately plunged into turbulent waters
where the currents of their respective religious and secular traditions
cross. There they stand, together with their daughters and students,
trying to keep their footing in the rough and murky waters churned
up by strong currents and countercurrents. With one hand, each

wants to steer her daughters and students to safe and gentle waters, while with the other, each grips her daughters' hands to hold them there, together, in the vortex. Miriam believes that fighting the current is the destiny of all women, whereas Elisheva believes that she is part of a transitional generation whose efforts will enable her daughter's generation to enjoy the still waters beyond the turbulence. None of the women, however, claims to have been forced into her present situation. They are where they are because that is where they think they ought to be. Even though each perceives her religious and cultural tradition as a patriarchy, each realizes, as well, that it is part of herself.

The women in this study have been struggling for most of their adult lives to inform their own religious lives with and to instill in the life of their communities values that might be considered indigenous to feminist culture—self-realization and the claiming of women's legitimate place in social life. Each believes that a religion that respects personal dignity and that hears and takes women's voices seriously is a religion more true to its calling. Still, the specific reforms that most of these women would like to see enacted are unacceptable to their respective religious authorities. It is clear that, at times, these women feel called on to make independent decisions about when to accede to and when to resist authority. They see themselves, in fact, as both agents of the continuity of tradition and of change. In other words, the empowered/powerless dichotomy does not exhaust all the alternatives of their situation. They know that change can be brought about formally only by the male authorities of their communities and hence that they themselves are virtually without official power. On the other hand, they know that the authorities are dependent on the community—including the women—to obey them. These women believe [or want to believe], therefore, that if, during their own lives and the lives of the younger generation whom they are socializing, they create new norms and new roles for women, the authorities will eventually acknowledge and ultimately accept these changes officially.

This long-term patience does not mean that these women do not feel frustrated in the short term by their lack of formal power. They often indicated that they would sidestep rabbinical or ecclesiastical authority if, for example, their daughters' psychological or "human" needs made that necessary. They fully realize that such a move would place them outside the bounds of organized religion. This realization means that, despite their commitment to their religious traditions, they accept and internalize the legitimacy of finding their own experience (see Taylor 1989). They reserve the right to alter their religious commitments should that prove necessary (under the most extreme of circumstances). While my interviews reveal their deep immersion in their cultures, the women want to claim that there are limits to the cultural/religious world with which they identify, that there is a dimension to mothering beyond their local culture and tradition, and that their mothering within a specific culture is somehow *optional*.[2]

There are times, Marianne says, when the dictates of religion and culture leave the maternal repertoire, times when "that mother thing kicks in." At those times, she says, she cannot see her children's lives in "black and white." However, for the most part, mothering in the way mandated by their religious context seemed optional to these women only in the sense that they knew about other options. Some even visited other options, tried different parishes and different religious affiliations, but a deep feeling emerged from most of their experiences that their religious tradition was their home. At times they felt oppressed by and even angry with their home, but it was theirs. Kathleen told me that when she complained about the Church, her daughter "would sometimes say . . . 'Well, if you're so upset with it all, why don't you become an Episcopalian?' I said that's because that is not who I am. I am a Catholic woman. This is who I am, and I will always be. It's the middle of me. So I can't change it, and there are no perfect places." Her religion was not an acquired attribute or habit; it defined who she was. Thus, although exit could be toyed with as a theoretical possibility, it was not a live option for her.[3] Moreover, she understood that "there are no perfect places" (a conclusion echoed by most of the women in their different contexts). The women understood that "secular humanism" offered no safe and neutral haven. They knew that every culture, including secular culture, is informed by a patriarchy, imbued with rules and regulations not necessarily authored by women or with women's best interests in mind. Kathleen continued, "Academia is not perfect, politics is not perfect, the world is not perfect, so why should I expect a human institution even if we believe it was instituted by God [to be perfect]? It's still filled with human beings. It cannot be perfect. However, I can work to do whatever I can to make it a little better."

Along very similar lines, Sandra said of the Catholic Church: "So as difficult as it is, I am saying we will join this club; but it doesn't mean we like golf. We use it for the pool or the dance floor. We believe in God and Jesus and his laws, but you know, we're here for the pool. The Church is just . . . one part of the patriarchy. There are many parts of the Church that are wonderful. If I quit every male-dominated institution in the world, I will be a hermit. It is all a matter of degree." Lucy emphasized in conversation the losses entailed by both staying in the Church and leaving it: "You don't have to leave the tradition in order to become yourself . . . It's a hard thing, and I never question those women who decide they can't do this, because I think it takes a toll. I do think, though, that there is a loss in walking away, and so I've always made the choice to stay, but it's a choice I make all the time. I'm choosing to do this, but I never question those who say, 'I've had enough.'"

Finally, Catherine told me that she stayed in the Church because there is realistic hope of reform. Referring to herself as a "post–Vatican II baby," she said: "I've seen so much change. I can see the hope. And I think that's what many of us keep holding onto and saying, 'If we all jump ship, nothing's ever going to change.' Some of us have to hold on. We can't just walk away from it. This is our community, and if we believe in what we need to try to do, then we have to stay and try to do it."

My most basic claims here have been that women mother within a culture and that personal identity is so deeply formed culturally that the role of a mother is inseparable from the role of cultural transmitter. But in the lives of these women and many others in similar situations, there is a complicating factor: they live, effectively, in more than one culture simultaneously. It is interesting that none of these women has found herself having to choose one set of cultural norms to the exclusion of the other. They tend to be acutely conscious of other options and of knowing other mothers who have opted for modern over traditional norms, and yet they can be eloquent in arguing the need for roots. As Seana puts it: "There is something wonderful about passing on to your children, because we have in a mixed culture like America a fractured sense of tradition. Everywhere we see people uprooted all the time. You wonder why children can't ground themselves or have no anchor or stability. It doesn't surprise me. So in an attempt to give [each of my daughters] some ground and some basis for rooting herself—it's at least some sense of legacy for our children."

Each woman I interviewed realizes, despite her belief in "anchor," "stability," or "rooting," that the decisions she makes in raising her adolescent daughters will often be obscured by the murkiness of the socio-cultural waters. Since "murkiness" is also an appropriate word to describe adolescence, some of these women believe that their daughters would prefer clarity and simplicity to the ambiguity of adolescence. But clarity and mothering do not easily go hand in hand, so the women face a dilemma. What of their own thoughts—their own reservations about tradition, their own modern educations—can they share these with their daughters? How can they help keep their daughters in the religious stream (as these mothers would clearly prefer) without their being carried off by the seductive clarity of a one-dimensional fundamentalism?

Here, my interviews show, the women were less than sure of themselves and adopted different solutions in response to their individual situations. Some adopted two distinct solutions: one for their daughters and another for their students. In other cases, there was a definite tendency to abdicate the role of socializer in order to resolve the conflict between being a mother and a socializer of adolescent girls. But during the course of the interviews, I saw an emerging pattern, a strategy for living with the conflicts between their roles as mothers and as socializers, and between their individual development as women and the dictates of their patriarchal cultures. To provide themselves with the sense of stability required to maintain their individuality in the face of strong traditions, the women appeared to engage in a dynamic, three-way balancing act. The structure of this triangle is formed by the main protagonists: mother, daughter, culture. One might say that the triangle represents the three sets of relationships between the protagonists, who may be reframed "I," "she," and "they." I may join with her or them, disturbing the equilibrium; stability is achieved when one of the three sides or relationships is parallel to the ground, in other words, when it is unchanging. When a state of stability is reached, the remaining sides may be modified freely without upsetting the structure's basic equilibrium. For example, given her daughter's conformity to the tradition, a mother might feel free to pursue a more unconventional religious way of life than she would if her daughter's loyalty were in doubt. Once the overall structure is secured by a solid "good girl" relationship between daughter and tradition, a mother can "afford" to intensify her connection with her daughter, while loosening her own connection with the tradition. A different scenario might be a firm relationship between mother and tradition such that her daughter can be more experimental and carefree about religion.

In choosing a metaphor or model capable of representing both stability and variability, I wish to emphasize two distinctive features of the lives of the women I interviewed: the persistence of unresolved tensions between conflicting values and aspirations, and the elimination—or the attenuation—of some of these tensions by means of compromises that the overall stability of their socio-cultural frameworks made possible.

Some of the psychological theories of mother-daughter relationships portray daughters as threats to their mothers.[4] According to these theories, mothers envy their daughters because their daughters have choices that they—as mothers and as wives—don't have[5]; or else, mothers envy their daughters' budding sexuality, which reminds them of their waning sexuality.[6] Other theories depict a cyclical pattern of oppression where mothers who were victims of an oppressive patriarchy victimize their own daughters and unwittingly carry out the dictates of the father's law (see Kaplan 1992). In addition, there are theories that depict mothers as benevolent jailers who guard their daughters by restricting their choices in order to protect them from having to pay the heavy price the community exacts for bad behavior (cf. Dinnerstein 1976).

The rhetoric of the women I interviewed revealed that their legitimacy as good mothers was tied up with their daughters' behavior.[7] If their daughters were rebellious and cast off tradition, the mothers could no longer act freely as resisters to that tradition. A daughter who leaves the religious community casts a "not good enough" shadow on her mother, thereby impugning both her religious character and her mothering.

The women's investment in being "good enough mothers" is sufficient to make them go along with community norms even when they believe that some of these norms are problematic. This was most noticeable in the decisions Jewish women made about how to celebrate their daughters' *bat mitzvahs*. For most of the women, conforming with community standards was safer than encouraging their daughters to act independently by, say, publicly reading from the Torah (not "the norm" for women in their communities). Their realignment with community norms seemed to confirm them as mothers of "normal" daughters. While it would clearly be an overstatement to describe these women, either Jewish or Catholic, as slaves of the patriarchy, it is true that they silence a part of themselves insofar as they do not speak entirely freely with their daughters about their views on religion, their roles as women within their tradition, or their beliefs about the relationship between their religious and secular concerns. I suggest that the women choose to ignore parts of themselves in order to maintain their positions in relation to their tradition. Yet, despite their reticence, they very much want their daughters to know about their views, and, in fact, some of them are convinced their daughters know their thoughts even if they do not voice them. They seem to believe in what Sara Ruddik calls a "mother tongue" ("the women's way of connecting"), which daughters, and students as well, understand in the absence of articulation. For instance, Lucy told me that "without [my] making a statement, I think [my students] knew that I was working hard to change [certain policies]."

Still, though these mothers would very much like to believe in a theory of "maternal silences" where "what is unspeakable may nevertheless be heard" (Hirsch 1989, p. 27), they invariably have to face the fact that what is not spoken is usually not heard. Elizabeth put the matter succinctly: "I question . . . if I disappeared tomorrow, what would she think I thought of the Catholic religion. I'm not sure what she would think." Yehudit, also concerned that her daughter does not truly know her, said, "The fact is that I would like her to at least hear me once [teach a class]. This is necessary in order to know what I am about at all. When I am gone, I would like her to remember something." The "mother tongue" these women believed in was more complex than they would have liked.

A most serious dilemma for these women is their relationship with the tradition. There is a value to the tradition for themselves and for their daughters, and they cannot and do not want to separate themselves from it. They express anguish at the idea of leaving their traditions, a price that would be almost unbearable. In initiating their daughters into womanhood in their respective orthodoxies, these women know they must in a deep way split from their daughters. A curtain inevitably rises between them and their daughters. Their daughters cannot fully know their own mothers. It seems to me that when a *mechitza* divides men and women in the synagogue, what follows is a *mechitza* between generations of women. The women interviewed gave voice to this particular painful price that patriarchy demands—that daughters cannot know their own mothers.

The women who send their daughters to schools that are more conservative than those they teach in offer a variety of explanations. Some admit to acquiescing to an external standard imposed by a husband or by the community. Others simply say that they want their daughters to receive the clear and unambiguous indoctrination in traditional and communal values that they themselves cannot provide. They fear that if the message their daughters receive is not clear enough, then legitimate, socially acceptable resistance may turn into illegitimate, unacceptable rebellion—the dynamic balance between protagonists may collapse, at a very high price. Rather than expose their daughters to the pain of social exclusion and isolation, these women choose to protect them by offering a safe, traditional religious education. Yet, none of these women saw herself as actively silencing her daughters. Were the girls to express doubts, or voice personal questions about their traditions, such talk and thinking would be encouraged. Even the women who did not share their thoughts and their own reservations with their daughters were confident that their daughters knew that their mothers were resisters within the community and were prepared to discuss these issues, if asked.

The questions, How do you speak to your daughter? How do you educate her? What do you share with her, and what do you keep silent about? What part of your community's ideology and values do you openly accept, and what do you reject?—struck a chord with women in widely varying contexts.[8] They responded to them as some of the deepest questions that a mother of girls can face. I have been careful, throughout, to refrain from the assertion that mothers universally face the same dilemmas[9] or even the same questions.[10] What I have done instead is to inform women who are mothering in different cultures what the range of answers to my inquiries has been and then to record their responses. The cross-cultural empathy that was my reward for this contextualist methodology was often deeply moving. Passages from interviews with Jewish women brought forth from the Catholic women profound feelings of empathy with what they perceived as a common struggle to achieve a balance among their commitments as mothers. But it was the quite pronounced differences in their respective religious cultural traditions that gave rise to these expressions of solidarity. It was their rootedness in their respective particularisms that enabled respect for the particularisms of others.

All mothers mother in an orthodoxy, or a set of entangled orthodoxies, that entail a set or sets of shoulds. That is the given. The challenge is raising a daughter under these circumstances, as any of the women I interviewed for this book will attest. Contiguous orthodoxies are rarely independent of each other, at times overlap, and very often conflict. Mothers are constantly making choices that satisfy one orthodoxy and outrage another. They hear these conflicting voices as voices of their own, as internal voices, and they respond, at best, with a difficult negotiation among options and, often enough, with what psychologists call "splitting." Some voices are perceived as coming from outside ("You always this!" "You never that!"). It is difficult enough as an individual to live with such differing and often opposing convictions. When a mother is in the demanding process of initiating a daughter into womanhood, however, metaphors such as "I am of two minds" seem overwhelmingly literal. The experience of divorce from one orthodoxy or another is like evacuating one of those minds, and in any case, as Kathleen told me, there are no perfect places. In which case, we should have no expectation of perfect mothers. The most a mother can hope for—and it is quite a challenge—is to be able to handle the complexity of equally compelling options without vertigo. When asked how they bring off this daily miracle, the women I interviewed tended to talk about abdications, negotiations, delegations, coalitions, commitments, self-silencing, protecting, compartmentalizing, and resistance. And when the conflict is of the most ominous kind, when "culture" conflicts with the "nonnegotiable core" of their identity, then, as Marianne put it, "that mother thing kicks in." Whatever the mother thing is or is not, it seems to be a woman's ally when her daughters seem most likely to be at risk. But perhaps it is not her only ally. Sometimes there is a daughter thing that kicks in as well.

Notes · References · Index

 *Notes*

1. *"I Think I'm of Two Minds"*

1. The *mechitza* exists so that there is a separation during prayers between men and women.
2. See Ruddick 1989, Chodorow and Contratto 1989, Orbach and Eichenbaum 1993, Groen 1993.
3. In *Mothering against the Odds,* the authors preface their book by saying, "[T]he voices of mothers, speaking of their (our) own subjective experiences, are not being heard or well represented in the mainstream cultural discourses of psychological development, clinical practice or social policy . . . [O]ur lived reality seemed missing from the dominant ideologies reflected in current 'expert knowledge'" (García Coll, Surrey, Weingarten 1998, pp. xv–xvi). Maureen Reddy, Martha Roth, and Amy Sheldon comment that "oddly enough, readers of feminist literature seldom discover the voices of feminist mothers speaking as mothers. Usually mothers are objects of analysis as feminists, too, replicate the nonconformist interest in mothers chiefly as objects of their children's demands . . . This collection seeks to shift the focus of attention from daughters to mothers" (1994, p. 1). Karen Horney as early as 1937 held that this disregard of cultural factors "is the main reason why psychoanalysis, inasmuch as it faithfully follows the theoretical paths beaten by Freud, seems in spite of its seemingly boundless potentialities to have

come into a blind alley, manifesting itself in a rank growth of abstruse theories and the use of a shadowy terminology" (Horney 1937, p. 21).

4. Freud, for example, called attention to one aspect of the mother-daughter relationship: "After puberty the mother takes up the duty of protecting her daughter's chastity" (1931, p. 201). After Freud, many psychological theorists charged this relationship with specific meaning and purpose. Women had to make sense of the task, whether as a description or a prescription, of educating their daughters on the prevailing notions of female goodness. Mothers became, then, their daughters' jailers and oppressors; they were represented by these theorists as women who repressed their daughters' natural development and silenced their voices. They were blamed if they repressed and equally called to task if they didn't. They were judged by how their daughters behaved.

5. "The observer, therefore, must attempt to see the symbols from the standpoint of the culture, rather than imposing on them the frameworks and understandings of other cultures within which the same symbols may have different meanings" (Woods 1996, pp. 39–40).

6. I recognized the possibility that it "may neither be feasible nor possible to harmonize observer and insider perspectives so as to achieve a consensus about 'ethnographic truth'" (Angrosino and Mays de Perez 2000, p. 678).

7. I analyzed the narratives primarily according to the guidelines of *A Guide to Reading Narrative of Conflict and Choice for Self and Moral Voice* (Brown et al. 1988), which enabled me to enter the data several ways, attending each time to the different voices and themes that emerged during the interviews.

8. See, for example, S. Freud 1931; A. Freud 1958; Mahler 1968, 1975; Blos 1963; and Erikson, 1950, 1968.

9. According to psychoanalytic theory, a primary goal of development is *individuation,* an emotional separation from the child's first "love object"—the mother: "The turning away from the mother is a most important step in the little girl's development" (S. Freud 1931, p. 207). This separation is held to recur at various points in the developmental life cycle. The ability to separate, to individuate, from one's mother at

the "appropriate" time is said to be an important factor in mental health, and a necessary condition for developing independence and the capacity to engage in mature intimate relationships.

Motherhood offers women the opportunity to achieve partial redemption from the inferiority that they are bound to feel, according to Freud. According to Helene Deutch, "the mother's sacrifice is also made easy by the fact that through the child, especially if it is a male child, she compensates for the one great lack of her life, the lack of a penis" (Suleiman 1985, p. 353).

10. Members of the Stone Center struggled with whether in their position of mutuality they did not idealize relationships. They address this question directly in "Some Misconceptions and Reconceptions of a Relational Approach." They say, "An empathic approach, by definition, does not mean idealizing. Idealizing is creating a falsity . . . An empathic approach means the attempt to be with the truth of the other person's experience in all of its aspects . . . [I]t has to mean to be with the difficult, conflictual, and destructive feelings and thoughts that we all experience. But it also means being with the strengths and potential strengths as well" (Miller, Jordan, Kaplan, Stiver, and Surrey 1997, p. 27).

11. Kathy Weingarten, Janet Surrey, and Cynthia García Coll claim that "all the contributors to this book share the belief that mother blaming—and the ubiquitous splitting of mothers and mothering into good and bad, right and wrong, that underlies it—has exerted a powerful and destructive influence on family life" (1998, p. 3).

12. See Ladd-Taylor and Umansky 1998, p. 4; also see Caplan 1989; Welldon 1988; Thurer 1994.

13. Torah study has been the most important aspect of traditional Jewish culture since at least the first century C.E. It is more than an intellectual pursuit; it represents a primary religious moment of intimate encounter with divine revelation. Becoming a scholar of Torah, which in practice means Talmud, has been the highest religious aspiration. It is no wonder, therefore, that the scholar is the main figure of authority in the Orthodox Jewish community. The institution of the yeshiva—an

intense, all-encompassing educational environment—was created to produce and nurture this ideal type. The yeshiva has been not only the supreme institution of higher learning but also constitutive of the communal leadership, especially of the intellectual elite (see Halbertal and Hartman Halbertal 1998). Because of the unparalleled importance of this ideal in the tradition, it is crucial to consider the exclusion of women from yeshiva life, which is perhaps analogous to the denial of citizenship to women in the Greek polis, where the life of the active citizen was regarded as the highest fulfillment of human potential. The justification of the prohibition against teaching women Torah extends beyond formal legal reasoning into the domain of myth and ideology. The Halakhic ban on teaching women the Oral Law reflects and reinforces a specific psychological portrait of women, which for generations has provided the ideological rationalization for this policy. Women are seen as the "weaker sex" particularly in terms of their intellectual limitations and sexual proclivities. The stereotypical woman is the victim of her passionate nature. She is vain, sexually vulnerable, and inherently incapable (because of her female "essence") of mastering the intellectual and spiritual disciplines necessary for pursuing the ideal of Torah scholarship. See *Babylonian Talmud,* Tractate Sota: 20a; Maimonides (*Mishneh Torah:* Laws Concerning the Study of Torah, I:13); and *Babylonian Talmud,* Tractate Kiddushin: 70b.

14. For an overview of laws concerning sexuality in Judaism, see Greenberg 1990.

15. For an overview of Roman Catholic teachings on sexuality see Porcile-Santiso (1990) and Ruether (1990).

16. Gilligan 1988, 1990a and b, 1997; Gilligan, Brown, and Rogers 1990.

17. Carol Gilligan comments, "Suddenly girls feel the presence of a standard which does not come out of their experience and an image which, because embodied, calls into question the reality which they have lived in—the moving, changing world of thoughts and feelings, relationships and people . . . What once seemed ordinary to girls—speaking, differences, anger, conflict, fighting, bad as well as good thoughts and feelings, now seems treacherous: laced with danger, a sign of imperfection, a harbinger of being left out, not chosen" (1990, p. 32).

2. *Ritual Observance and Religious Learning*

1. See B. Venarde 1997, C. Walker Bynum 1992, P. Johnson 1991, B. Newman 1987, and G. Daichman 1986.

3. *Abdications and Coalitions*

1. I will be using components of the "reading for self" method as a way to help hear and understand the different ways the women I interviewed connect to their beliefs and culture. See Brown et al. (1988). This method aims at tuning the reader's/interpreter's ear to the multiple voices contained within an individual voice. See my discussion of Sima later in this chapter for a further example of this method.

2. J. Giele writes: "In Roger Gould's scheme, persons confront different aspects of their own arbitrary internal beliefs and inhibitions and gradually learn to question them. By age fifty most people will have shed all illusion of absolute safety given by rigid internal beliefs that came from childhood. They will then be freer than before to act as truly autonomous individuals" (1980, p. 154). One might interpret these women's questioning in this light; however, I would not automatically describe religious beliefs as "rigid" or "arbitrary." The women to whom I spoke are questioning people who do not believe they have all the answers.

3. Carol Gilligan (1995) distinguishes between a feminine and a feminist ethos. A feminine "ethic of care rests on a faulty notion of relationships" (p. 125) and is based on the ideal of selflessness; a feminist ethos involves relationships that do not entail a woman's being "out of relation" with herself. It is the latter ethos that some of the women expressed with regard to their daughters.

4. The only birth control that is officially sanctioned is the natural rhythm method: "If, then, there are serious motives to space our births, which derive from the physical or psychological conditions of husband and wife, or from external conditions, the Church teaches that it is then licit to take into account the natural rhythms immanent in the generative

functions, for the use of marriage in the infecund periods only, and in this way to regulate birth without offending the moral principles which have been recalled earlier." *Encyclical Letter of His Holiness: On the Regulation of Birth* (1968).

5. "In conformity with these landmarks in the human and Christian vision of marriage, we must once again declare that the direct interruption of the generative process already begun, and, above all, directly willed and procured abortion, even if for therapeutic reasons, are to be absolutely excluded as licit means of regulating birth . . . In truth, if it is sometimes licit to tolerate a lesser evil in order to avoid a greater evil or to promote a greater good, it is not licit even for the gravest reasons, to do evil, so that good may follow therefrom." Ibid., pp. 18–19.

4. Teaching

1. One of the major figures of ultra-Orthodoxy, the Hafetz Hayim, makes the following observation about the changes in society that justify adopting a new attitude toward the education of women: "It would seem to be that this [prohibition against female education] is only valid at those times of history when people lived in the same place as their ancestors and the ancestral tradition was very strong and individuals were motivated to act in the manner of [their] forefathers . . . Nowadays, however, when the tradition of our fathers has been weakened and people no longer live close to their parental environment and especially when there are many people who have received secular education, certainly it is required to teach them the entire Bible, the ethical writings of our sages, etc., so that the principles of our holy faith will be strong for them. Otherwise, Heaven forbid, they may deviate entirely from the path of God and violate the precepts of the Torah." (*Likutei Halakhot* to *Sota* 20a). The Hafetz Hayim thus described the conditions of modernity that justified changing the traditional policy toward women's education. The intimate household environment with its traditional ethos and forms of social bonding were undermined by the greater mobility and dispersion of populations in the modern era. Also, the growing participation of women in secular education created a dangerous asymmetry with their

deficient Torah education. In response to these modern conditions, this Halakhic authority recommended a change in Jewish education by introducing women to Bible learning and ethical education. The Hafetz Hayim did not authorize the study of Talmud for women. The study of Talmud, to this day, remains the exclusive prerogative of males in ultra-Orthodox circles. In some modern Orthodox settings, settings in which the women in this study teach, however, the study of Talmud by women has been introduced both at high school and university levels with the endorsement of a number of rabbinic authorities.

5. *The Conflict of Dogmas*

1. I often wonder how much of mothering in modern Western culture is influenced by trying to anticipate how your child's therapist will judge you in the future.
2. Gluck and Patai (1991) refer to these recurring kinds of statements as "key phrases": "[These phrases] aim to define a type of relation between the self and the social sphere, that is, the community, and more broadly, the society as a whole. The key phrase then expresses the harmony, the indifference, the ambiguity, the conflict, and so on, existing between self and society" (p. 79).
3. Nervous *chalerias* is a (half Yiddish) term meaning a hysterical type of person.
4. See J. B. Miller (1976) for an analysis of different kinds of conflict, such as "covert conflict" and "overt conflict."
5. According to tradition, the Hebrews escaping from Egypt remained in the desert for forty years so that a new generation could be born in real freedom, free of the crippling slave mentality of their parents.

6. *"No Perfect Places"*

1. In fact, Gilligan (1994) says, "People's voices flow in and out of one another, carrying psychology and also culture, mixing inner and outer worlds" (p. 22).

2. See Ruddick (1989), "Part II: Protection Nurturance and Training."

3. Whether to stay within a religion while trying to reinterpret aspects of it or to leave traditional religion has been a focus of much discussion among feminist religious theologians. See, for example, Hampson (1990 and 1996), Schüssler Fiorenza (1992, 1998), Trible (1984) about the Christian faith; and Adler (1998), Heschel (1983), and Plaskow (1990, 1998), regarding Judaism.

4. See Deutch (1944); Friday (1977); Welldon (1988).

5. Fox-Genovese (1996) says: "It is as if mothers unconsciously see clothes as a way of retaining control of their daughters—of keeping them girls rather than facing them as independent women. Certainly, I now believe that concern about my emerging sexuality motivated my own mother's hostility to my elegant—and revealing—straight skirt (pp. 49–50).

6. Flaake comments, "From the mother's perspective the bodily development of her daughter confronts her with the upcoming separation and her own aging process. It can remind the mother of her own unsatisfied sexuality, her own unfulfilled desire for autonomy, and her own problems with femininity" (Flaake 1993, p. 9). Flaake goes on to cite R. Waldeck who claims that "In our culture, the mother's envy of her daughter, including the wide range of options available to her as a young woman today can be linked to the predominant views on menstruation which leave the daughter with the message: 'Your life is before you. You are young and beautiful, but that which makes you a woman is dirty and has to be hidden'" (Waldeck 1988, pp. 342–343).

7. Their rhetoric reveals a "learned" phenomenon about how mothers are judged. For example, Sarah Bruckner (1994) says: "Mothers are judged by whether their children's hair is brushed, socks are matched, noses are wiped. Strangers in malls feel empowered, and apparently compelled, to applaud ("Your daughters are so well-behaved!") or hiss ("You shouldn't let them have lollipops, you know")" (p. 35).

8. Fox-Genovese writes, "What remains striking is how much women of different backgrounds and ages have in common. It is rare for one woman to talk to another for more than a few minutes without stumbling on something that leads to a heartfelt: 'I know just how you feel'" (Fox-Genovese 1996, pp. 152–153).

9. Recent theorists of methodology have revisited the issue concerning the meaning and possible applicability of "reliability" and "validity" in qualitative research (Merrick 1999). Geertz (1973) suggested we use the term "anticipate" rather than "predict."

10. I followed Brown and Gilligan's (1992) methodology in analyzing their interviews with adolescent girls: "Our claim, therefore, in presenting this work is not that the girls we spoke with are representative of all girls or some ideal sample of girls, but rather that we learned from this group of girls and young women, and what we discovered seemed worthy of others' attention" (p. 23).

 *References*

Adler, R. 1998. *Engendering Judaism: An Inclusive Theology and Ethics.* Philadelphia: Jewish Publication Society.

Angrosino, M. V., and K. A. Mays de Perez. 2000. "Rethinking Observation." In N. K. Denzin and Y. S. Lincoln, eds., *Handbook of Qualitative Research,* 2d ed. Thousand Oaks, Calif.: Sage Publications.

Apter, T. 1990. *Altered Loves: Mothers and Daughters during Adolescence.* New York: Ballantine Books.

Biale, R. 1984. *Women and Jewish Law.* New York: Schocken Books.

Blos, P. 1963. *On Adolescence: A Psychoanalytic Interpretation.* New York: Free Press.

Bordo, S. 1993. *Unbearable Weight: Feminism, Western Culture, and the Body.* Berkeley: University of California Press.

Brown, L., D. Argyris, D. Attanucci, B. Barduge, C. Gilligan, K. Johnson, B. Miller, D. Osborne, J. Ward, G. Wiggins, and D. Wilcox. 1988. *A Guide to Reading Narratives of Conflict and Choice for Self and Moral Voice.* Monograph no. 1. Harvard Project on Women's Psychology and Girls' Development. Cambridge, Mass.: Harvard Graduate School of Education.

Brown, L., and C. Gilligan. 1992. *Meeting at the Crossroads: Women's Psychology and Girl's Development.* Cambridge, Mass.: Harvard University Press.

Bruckner, S. 1994. "Two Moms, Two Kids, and a Dog." In M. Reddy, M. Roth, and A. Sheldon, eds., *Mother Journeys: Feminists Write about Mothering.* Minneapolis: Spinsters Ink.

Bynum, C. W. 1992. *Fragmentation and Redemption: Essays on Gender and the Human Body in Medieval Religion.* New York: Zone Books.

Caplan, P. 1989. *Don't Blame Mother.* New York: Harper & Row.

————. 1998. "Mother Blaming." In M. Ladd-Taylor and L. Umansky, eds., *"Bad" Mothers: The Politics of Blame in Twentieth-Century America.* New York: New York University Press.

Chodorow, N. 1978. *The Reproduction of Motherhood.* Berkeley: University of California Press.

————. 1994. *Femininities, Masculinities, Sexualities: Freud and Beyond.* Lexington: University Press of Kentucky.

————. 1995. "Gender as a Personal and Cultural Construction." *Signs* 20(3): 517–542.

————. 1999. *The Power of Feelings: Personal Meaning in Psychoanalysis, Gender, and Culture.* New Haven: Yale University Press.

Chodorow, N., and S. Contratto. 1989. "The Fantasy of the Perfect Mother." In N. Chodorow, ed., *Feminism and Psychoanalytic Theory.* New Haven: Yale University Press.

Coll, R. 1998. *Christianity and Feminism in Conversation.* Mystic, Conn.: Twenty-Third Publications.

Daichman, G. S. 1986. *Wayward Nuns in Medieval Literature.* Syracuse: Syracuse University Press.

Deutsch, H. 1944. *The Psychology of Women.* New York: Grune & Stratton.

Dillon, M. 1999. *Catholic Identity: Balancing Reason, Faith, and Power.* Cambridge: Cambridge University Press.

Dinnerstein, D. 1976. *The Mermaid and the Minotaur.* New York: Harper & Row.

Ellinson, G. 1992. *The Modest Way.* Israel: Department for Torah Education and Culture in the Diaspora of the World Zionist Organization.

El-Or, T. 1994. *Educated and Ignorant: Ultra Orthodox Jewish Women and Their World.* Boulder, Colo.: Lynne Rienner.

————. 2002. *Next Year I Will Know More: Literacy and Identity among Young Orthodox Women in Israel.* Detroit: Wayne State University Press.

Erikson, E. 1950. *Childhood and Society.* New York: W. W. Norton and Co.

———. 1968. *Identity: Youth and Crisis.* New York: W. W. Norton and Co.

Fine, M. 1992. *Disruptive Voices: The Possibilities of Feminist Research.* Ann Arbor: University of Michigan Press.

Flaake, K. 1993. "A Body of One's Own: Sexual Development and the Female Body in the Mother-Daughter Relationship." In J. Mens-Verhulst, K. Schreurs, and L. Woertman, eds., *Daughtering and Mothering: Female Subjectivity Reanalysed.* New York: Routledge.

Fontana, A., and J. Frey. 2000. "The Interview: From Structured Questions to Negotiated Text." In N. K. Denzin and Y. S. Lincoln, eds., *Handbook of Qualitative Research,* 2nd ed. Thousand Oaks: Sage Publications.

Fox-Genovese, E. 1996. *Feminism Is Not the Story of My Life.* New York: Bantam Doubleday Dell Publishing Group.

Freud, A. 1930a. "Infantile Amnesia and the Oedipus Complex." In *The Writings of Anna Freud: Introduction to Psychoanalysis.* New York: International Universities Press.

———. 1930b. "The Latency Period." In *The Writings of Anna Freud: Introduction to Psychoanalysis.* New York: International Universities Press.

———. 1958. "Adolescence." In *The Psychoanalytic Study of the Child.* Vol. 13. New York: International Universities Press.

Freud, S. 1931. "Female Sexuality." In S. Freud, *Sexuality and the Psychology of Love.* New York: Collier Books.

Friday, N. 1977. *My Mother/My Self: The Daughter's Search for Identity.* New York: Delacorte.

Gadamer, H. G. 1986. *Truth and Method.* New York: Continuum.

Gall, M., W. Borg, and J. Gall. 1996. *Educational Research: An Introduction.* New York: Longman Publishers.

García Coll, C., J. Surrey, and K. Weingarten, eds. 1998. *Mothering against the Odds: Diverse Voices of Contemporary Mothers.* New York: Guilford Press.

Gardner, H. L. 1959. *The Business of Criticism.* Oxford: Clarendon Press.

Geertz, C. 1973. *Local Knowledge: Further Essays in Interpretive Anthropology.* New York: Basic Books.

———. 1986. "The Uses of Diversity." In Sterling M. McMurrin, eds., *The Tanner Lectures on Human Values,* vol. 24. Salt Lake City: University of Utah Press.

————. 2000. *Available Light: Anthropological Reflections on Philosophical Topics*. Princeton: Princeton University Press.

Giele, J. 1980. "Adulthood as Transcendence of Age and Sex." In N. Smegler and E. Erikson, eds., *Themes of Workhood and Love in Adulthood*. Cambridge: Harvard University Press.

Gilligan, C. 1979. "Woman's Place in a Man's Life Cycle." *Harvard Educational Review* 49 (4): 431–444.

————. 1988. "Exit Voice Dilemmas in Adolescent Development." In C. Gilligan, J. Ward, and J. Taylor, eds., *Mapping the Moral Domain*. Cambridge: Harvard University Press.

————. 1990a. "Joining the Resistance: Psychology, Politics, Girls, and Women." *Michigan Quarterly Review* 29 (4).

————. 1990b. "Teaching Shakespeare's Sister: Notes from the Underground of Female Adolescence." In C. Gilligan, N. P. Lyons, and T. Hanmer, *Making Connections: The Relational Worlds of Adolescent Girls at Emma Willard School*. Cambridge: Harvard University Press.

————. 1994. "Getting Civilized." *Fordham Law Review* 63 (1): 17–31.

————. 1995. "Hearing the Difference: Theorizing Connection." *Hypatia* 10 (2): 120–126.

————. 1997. "Remembering Iphigenia: Voice, Resonance, and a Talking Cure." In E. Shapiro, ed., *The Inner World in the Outer World: Psychodynamic Perspectives*. New Haven: Yale University Press.

Gilligan, C., L. M. Brown, and A. Rogers. 1990. "Psyche Embedded: A Place for Body, Relationships, and Culture in Personality Theory." In A. Rabin, R. Zucker, R. Emmons, and S. Frank, eds., *Studying Persons and Lives*. New York: Springer.

Gluck, S. B., and D. Patai, eds. 1991. *Women's Words: The Feminist Practice of Oral History*. New York: Routledge.

Gould, R. 1980. "Transformations during Early and Middle Adult Years." In N. Smegler and E. Erikson, eds., *Themes of Workhood and Love in Adulthood*. Cambridge: Harvard University Press.

Greeley, A. 1990. *The Catholic Myth: The Behavior and Beliefs of American Catholics*. New York: Macmillan Publishing Co.

Greenberg, B. 1990. "Female Sexuality and Bodily Functions in the Jewish Tradition." In J. Becher, ed., *Women, Religion and Sexuality*. Philadelphia: Trinity Press International.

Groen, M. 1993. "Mother-Daughter, The 'Black Continent': Is a Multicultural Future Possible?" In J. Mens-Verhulst, K. Schreurs, and L. Woertman, eds., *Daughtering and Mothering: Female Subjectivity Reanalysed.* New York: Routledge.

Halbertal, M. and T. Hartman Halbertal. 1998. "The Yeshiva." In A. Rorty, ed., *Philosophers on Education: New Historical Perspectives.* London, New York: Routledge Press.

Hampson, D. 1990. *Theology and Feminism.* Cambridge: Blackwell Publishers.

———. 1996. *After Christianity.* Pennsylvania: Trinity Press International.

Herman, J., and H. Lewis. 1989. "Anger in the Mother-Daughter Relationship." In T. Bernay and D. Cantor, eds., *The Psychology of Today's Woman: New Psychoanalytic Visions.* Cambridge: Harvard University Press.

Heschel, S. 1983. *On Being a Jewish Feminist.* New York: Shocken Books.

Hirsch, M. 1989. *The Mother/Daughter Plot: Narrative, Psychoanalysis, Feminism.* Indianapolis: Indiana University Press.

Horney, K. 1937. *The Neurotic Personality of Our Time.* New York: Norton.

Irigaray, L. 1993. *Je, tu, nous: Toward a Culture of Difference.* Trans. A. Martin. New York: Routledge.

John Paul II 1995. *Letter of Pope John Paul II to Women.* Vatican City.

Johnson, P. D. 1991. *Equal in Monastic Profession: Religious Women in Medieval France.* Chicago: University of Chicago Press.

Jones, K. W. 1998. "'Mother Made Me Do It': Mother-Blaming and the Women of Child Guidance." In M. Ladd-Taylor and L. Umansky, eds., *"Bad" Mothers: The Politics of Blame in Twentieth-Century America.* New York: New York University Press.

Jordan, J., A. Kaplan, J. B. Miller, I. Stiver, and J. Surrey. 1991. *Women's Growth in Connection: Writings from the Stone Center.* New York: The Guilford Press.

Josselson, R. 1987. *Finding Herself: Pathways to Identity Development in Women.* San Francisco: Jossey Bass Publishers.

Kaplan, E. A. 1992. *Motherhood and Representation: The Mother in Popular Culture and Melodrama.* London: Routledge.

Ladd-Taylor, M. and L. Umansky. 1998. "Introduction." In M. Ladd-Taylor and L. Umansky, eds., *"Bad" Mothers: The Politics of Blame in Twentieth-Century America.* New York: New York University Press.

LeVine, R. 1990. "Infant Environments in Psychoanalysis: A Cross-Cultural View." In J. Stigler, R. Shweder, and G. Herdt, *Cultural Psychology: Essays on Comparative Human Development*. New York: Cambridge University Press.

LeVine, R., and P. Miller. 1990. "Commentary." *Human Development* 33 (1): 73–80.

Levi-Strauss, C. 1972. *Structural Anthropology*. Trans. C. Jacobson. Harmondsworth: Penguin.

Lieblich, A., R. Tuval-Mashiach, and T. Zilber. 1998. *Narrative Research: Reading, Analysis, and Interpretation*. Applied Social Research Methods Series, Vol. 47. Thousand Oaks, Calif.: Sage Publications.

Lomsky-Feder, E. 1996. "A Woman Studies War: Stranger in a Man's World." In R. Josselson, ed., *The Narrative Study of Lives*. Thousand Oaks, Calif.: Sage Publications.

Mahler, M. 1968. "On Human Symbiosis and the Vicissitudes of Individuation." In *Infantile Psychosis*. Vol. 1. New York: International Universities Press.

Mahler, M., F. Pine, and A. Bergman. 1975. *The Psychological Birth of the Human Infant*. New York: Basic Books.

McDonnell, J. T. 1998. "On Being the 'Bad' Mother of an Autistic Child." In M. Ladd-Taylor and L. Umansky, eds., *"Bad" Mothers: The Politics of Blame in Twentieth-Century America*. New York: New York University Press.

Meiselman, M. 1978. *Jewish Woman in Jewish Law*. New York: Ktav Publishing House.

Merrick, E. 1999. "An Exploration of Quality in Qualitative Research: Are Reliability and Validity Relevant?" In M. Kopala and L. A. Suzuki, eds., *Using Qualitative Methods in Psychology*. Thousand Oaks, Calif.: Sage.

Miller, J. B. 1976. *Toward a New Psychology of Women*. Boston: Beacon Press.

Miller, J. B., J. Jordan, A. Kaplan, I. Stiver, and J. Surrey. 1997. "Some Misconceptions and Reconceptions of a Relational Approach." In J. Jordan, ed., *Women's Growth in Diversity: More Writings from the Stone Center*. New York: Guilford Press.

Newman, B. 1987. *Sister of Wisdom: St. Hildegard's Theology of the Feminine*. Berkeley: University of California Press.

Orbach, S., and L. Eichenbaum. 1993. "Feminine Subjectivity: Counter-transference and the Mother-Daughter Relationship." In J. Mens-Verhulst, K. Schreurs, and L. Woertman, eds., *Daughtering and Mothering: Female Subjectivity Reanalysed.* New York: Routledge.

Paul VI. 1968. *Encyclical Letter of His Holiness: On the Regulation of Birth.* Vatican City.

Plaskow, J. 1990. *Standing Again at Sinai: Judaism from a Feminist Perspective.* New York: Harper.

———. 1998. "Transforming the Nature of Community: Toward a Feminist People of Israel." In P. Cooey, W. Eakin, and J. McDaniel Maryknoll, eds., *After Patriarchy: Feminist Transformations of the World Religions.* New York: Orbis Books.

Porcile-Santiso, M. T. 1990. "Roman Catholic Teachings on Female Sexuality." In J. Becher, ed., *Women, Religion and Sexuality.* Philadelphia: Trinity Press International.

Reddy, M. T., M. Roth, and A. Sheldon. 1994. *Mother Journeys: Feminists Write about Mothering.* Minneapolis: Spinsters Ink.

Ruddick, S. 1989. *Maternal Thinking.* New York: Ballantine Books.

Ruether, R. R. 1990. "Catholicism, Women, Body and Sexuality: A Response." In J. Becher, *Women, Religion and Sexuality.* Philadelphia: Trinity Press International.

Schüssler Fiorenza, E. 1992. *But She Said: Feminist Practices of Biblical Interpretation.* Boston: Beacon Press.

———. 1998. *In Memory of Her: A Feminist Theological Reconstruction of Christian Origins.* New York: Crossroad.

Sciarra, D. 1999. "The Role of the Qualitative Researcher." In M. Kopala and L. A. Suzuki, eds. *Using Qualitative Methods in Psychology.* Thousand Oaks, Calif.: Sage.

Shkedi, A. 2002. (unpublished manuscript) "Multiple Populations in Qualitative Research."

Soloveichik, A. 1991. *Logic of the Heart, Logic of the Mind: Wisdom and Reflections on Topics of Our Times.* New York: Genesis Jerusalem Press.

Suleiman, S. R. 1985. "Writing and Motherhood." In S. Garner, C. Kahane, and M. Sprengnether, eds., *The (M)other Tongue: Essays in Feminist Psychoanalytic Interpretation.* Ithaca: Cornell University Press.

Taylor, C. 1989. *Sources of the Self: The Making of the Modern Identity.* Cambridge: Harvard University Press.

Thurer, S. L. 1994. "The Myths of Motherhood: How Culture Reinvents Motherhood." In M. Ladd-Taylor and L. Umansky, eds., *"Bad" Mothers: The Politics of Blame in Twentieth-Century America.* New York: New York University Press.

Trible, P. 1984. *Texts of Terror: Literary-Feminist Readings of Biblical Narratives.* Philadelphia: Fortress Press.

Venarde, B. L. 1997. *Women's Monasticism and Medieval Society: Nunneries in France and England, 890–1215.* Ithaca: Cornell University Press.

Waldeck, R. 1988. "Der rote Fleck in dunklen Kontinent," *Zeitschrift für Sexualforschung* 1: 189–205; and 2: 337–350.

Weingarten, K. 1998. "Sidelined No More: Promoting Mothers of Adolescents as a Resource for Their Growth and Development." In C. García Coll, I. J. Surrey, and K. Weingarten, eds., *Mothering against the Odds: Diverse Voices of Contemporary Mothers.* New York: The Guilford Press.

Weingarten, K., J. Surrey, C. Garcia-Coll, and M. Watkins. 1998. "Introduction." In C. García Coll, I. J. Surrey, and K. Weingarten, eds., *Mothering against the Odds: Diverse Voices of Contemporary Mothers.* New York: The Guilford Press.

Welldon, E. V. 1988. *Mother, Madonna, Whore: The Idealization and Denigration of Motherhood.* New York: Guilford Press.

Winnicott, D. W. 1986. *Home Is Where We Start From: Essays by a Psychoanalyst.* New York: Norton.

Woods, P. 1996. *Researching the Art of Teaching: Ethnography for Educational Use.* London: Routledge.

JEWISH SOURCES

Babylonian Talmud: Tractate Kiddushin: 33b–35b, 70b, Tractate Berachot: 20a–20b, Tractate Erubin: 96a–96b, Tractate Megillah: 23a, Tractate Sota: 20a, Tractate Ketubot: 62b–63a, Kol Bo: 73.

Maimonides, M. *Mishneh Torah:* The Laws of Fringes, 3,9; The Laws of

Kings, I,5; The Laws of Evidence, IX,1; The Laws Concerning the Study of Torah, I,13.

Meir Ha-Cohen, Israel (Hafetz Hayim). *Likutei Halakhot,* Sotah 20a p. 11b.

Rashi (Shlomo Yitzchaki): *Commentary to Tractate Avodah Zarah,* 18b.

Uziel, B. Z. M. 1984. *Piskei Uziel* (Rulings on Current Events). Jerusalem: Mosad ha-Rav Kook.

Index